THE DAWN OF AMERICAN METHODISM

Francis Asbury
From the oil-painting in the Wesleyan Mission House, London

THE
DAWN OF AMERICAN METHODISM

BY
RICHARD PYKE
AUTHOR OF
The Protestant Faith and Challenge,
Points for Protestants, etc.

WIPF & STOCK · Eugene, Oregon

Wipf and Stock Publishers
199 W 8th Ave, Suite 3
Eugene, OR 97401

The Dawn of American Methodism
By Pyke, Richard
Copyright©1933 Methodist Publishing - Epworth Press
ISBN 13: 978-1-5326-0029-6
Publication date 6/22/2016
Previously published by Epworth Press, 1933

TO MY WIFE

WHO JOURNEYED WITH ME IN AMERICA ; AND HAS BEEN
AN IDEAL FELLOW-TRAVELLER ON A MUCH
LONGER JOURNEY.

CONTENTS

CHAP.		PAGE
	PREFACE	9
	FOREWORD	11
I.	THE COUNTRY AND THE PEOPLE	13
II.	JOHN WESLEY IN AMERICA	21
III.	WHITEFIELD AND AMERICA	33
IV.	THE FIRST SOCIETIES	48
V.	PIONEERS	59
VI.	FRANCIS ASBURY AND THOMAS RANKIN	73
VII.	THE REVOLUTION	86
VIII.	THE SACRAMENTS AND ORDINATION	100
IX.	THE METHODIST EPISCOPAL CHURCH	113
X.	THE GENERAL CONFERENCE	126
XI.	TROUBLES AND TRIUMPHS	140
XII.	EVANGELISM AND EDUCATION	154
XIII.	THE SUNDERED CHURCH	166
	STATISTICS OF AMERICAN METHODISM TO-DAY	178
	INDEX	179

PREFACE

THE purpose of this outline is to introduce English readers to the story of the early days of Methodism in America. It is hardly necessary to say more, since the book can, and must, speak for itself. No one is more conscious than I am of the inadequate space given to many phases of the work : but perhaps no Englishman, and certainly no busy Methodist Minister, could ever deal exhaustively with the innumerable questions that arise, as one threads one's way through the rich, yet tangled story of such a movement.

A writer may offer excuse for obvious limitations ; but he has no right to expect indulgence, if he misrepresents the history he professes to relate. I have sought to verify my references, and to state the facts.

I have to acknowledge with gratitude my obligations to Dr. A. B. Cooke, the American Consul in Plymouth, who, as a member of the Methodist Episcopal Church South of America, has read my manuscript, and made valuable suggestions. This does not mean that he always endorses my opinions. Mrs. Leonard Pyke, B.A., has discovered imperfections which would otherwise have found their way into print.

10 THE DAWN OF AMERICAN METHODISM

I have also to thank the Rev. John Ford Reed for valuable suggestions, and my colleague, the Rev. W. Horswill, for the Index.

For a copy of Asbury's Journal I am indebted to the Rev. James Lewis, whose book on *Francis Asbury* has a cherished place on my shelves.

If what I have written gives a true picture of the origins of a great Church, and at the same time creates a desire to know still more, I shall have achieved my purpose.

R. PYKE.

PLYMOUTH, *June*, 1933.

FOREWORD

THE author of this book has accomplished a difficult and delicate task. He has condensed within a comparatively brief record the story of an historic era in Methodism, and he has done this without sacrificing any essential element of the story.

The book lays before its readers in broad lines the growth of Methodism in America from its beginning through the first round century of its history. But it is more than a mere historical record of events. No account of Methodism could be adequate that did not include biography as well as history; for the story of Methodism is above all else a record of individual lives. The author has been true to the record. He has been careful to give his readers an insight into the lives of the men and women who, through their sacrifice and heroism, were chiefly instrumental in laying the foundations of Methodism in America during stirring decades of colonization, of war, and of nation-building.

We have it on high authority that ' a good name is rather to be chosen than great riches.' Methodists would do well to remember the proverb of Solomon. The name they bear is a good one. Good, measured by every test—by the ideals for which it stands, by its influence, by the lives that have been cast into the making of it.

In olden time the heirs of a great lineage were spurred to high endeavour by the name they bore. *Noblesse oblige*, they said—our very name compels us.

We Methodists count in our lineage the names of Wesley and Whitefield, of Asbury and McKendree and Barbara Heck, with a host of men and women scarcely second to them in honour. These, our spiritual forbears, have by lives of sacrifice and devotion to high ideals won for their spiritual descendants the heritage of a good name. It is for us, heirs of that heritage, to say, as did those of olden time : *Noblesse oblige*—our very name compels us.

The Dawn of American Methodism should give Methodists everywhere a quickened sense of the priceless heritage that has been handed down to them in the name they bear. I wish it all success, with an ever-widening circle of readers.

A. B. COOKE.

AMERICAN CONSULATE,
   PLYMOUTH, ENGLAND.
     March 1, 1933.

THE DAWN OF AMERICAN METHODISM

CHAPTER I

THE COUNTRY AND THE PEOPLE

> ' The country, vexed by long winters and thinly peopled by warlike tribes of Indians, gave a rough welcome to the earlier colonists. After a fruitless attempt to form a settlement, Sir Humphrey Gilbert, one of the noblest spirits of his time, turned homewards again, to find his fate in the stormy seas. "We are as near to Heaven by sea as by land," were the famous words he was heard to utter, ere the light of his little bark was lost for ever in the darkness of the night.'—JOHN RICHARD GREEN—*A Short History of the English People.*

AT the time when Methodism was introduced to North America, there were in all thirteen British Colonies. These were sparsely populated with immigrants from England and their descendants. We have, of course, to remember that the original inhabitants were by no means excluded when the English arrived, though the advance of the immigrant meant generally a retirement of the Red Indians. A brief account of the country, the people, and the disposition of the religious forces at this time over such a wide area, should preface the story we have to tell.

It is probable that the existence of America had been known to uncultured tribes in Asia for thousands of years : but a belief may linger and decline until it degenerates into a fantastic legend, and is not seriously entertained by any one. This appears to have been the case with America. Daring seamen had visited the Continent five centuries before Columbus ; but having returned with their report of the land, and such features of it as their brief visit had revealed, the nine days' wonder survived only in half-forgotten records, or in stories which took their place with romance and fairy tales.

It was not until the fifteenth century that America secured a definite place in the records of our own country, and of Europe generally. That century, as we know, was marked by a spirit of restlessness and adventure. England, like some other European countries, bred a race of men to whom the stormy sea was a fascination, and any unexplored part of the world an irresistible magnet. These men were never so happy as when they were about to put forth from their own shores, to discover what lay beyond the dim wastes of an uncharted ocean. We may assent to such criticism as seems to have for its object a reduction of the moral stature of these adventurers, but we are compelled to admit that in them was the stern texture of which heroes are made. It may very well be, they believed, not only that they would discover a western route to India, or perchance light upon some undiscovered continent, but that they would return with every conceivable kind of treasure. With this they would both win the admiration of their country, and enrich themselves. Kingsley's blustering seaman, John Oxenham, is typical. In *Westward Ho!* he tells the Bideford people that he had seen ' a heap, seventy foot long, ten foot broad, and twelve foot high, of silver bars, and each bar

THE COUNTRY AND THE PEOPLE

between a thirty and forty pound weight . . . and more silver in Nombre de Dios than would pave all the streets in the West Country.'

It was on June 24, 1497, that John Cabot discovered Newfoundland, and proceeded to coast along the shores of North America. A year after, Columbus first saw the mainland. But even then, a hundred years had to pass before this new world came in any degree to be regarded as the possible home of a people who, for various reasons, might desire to leave their own country.

One of the most powerful of the reasons which induced Englishmen to venture across the sea, and try their fortunes in an unknown world, was the desire they had to secure a liberty of conscience and a freedom in worship, which James I and Laud denied them at home. England was a dangerous country for any man with firm religious convictions, which did not conform to the narrow views of the remorseless Laud. He and his monarch were determined to tune or coerce the consciences of all who showed any disagreement with their own love of power and inflexible regulations.

'I shall make them conform themselves,' said James I, 'or I will harry them out of the land.' He did his best to fulfil the threat. Westward Ho! therefore, threw its spell over the lovers of liberty. They knew they would sacrifice comfort, wealth, and it may be life itself, by thus venturing across the Atlantic; but no fears crushed their courage. It must be a lovely land, they felt, to which they were going, if going there they found freedom to worship God as their hearts desired.

The stream of emigrants increased in volume as

the years passed by. England could ill-afford to lose these sturdy souls. They were the very men and women to become the parents of a heroic race. That is what they did become : but who can believe that our own country was not sadly impoverished by their withdrawal ? They carried with them not only rugged personality and sterling qualities of character, they took also their possessions. Many of them were people of wealth, of education, and of good social standing. It is one of the unpleasant features of the tumultuous history of our country that at such a time a King, who has been spoken of as 'the wisest fool in Christendom,' and his son, whom Mr. Gladstone described as 'a dreadful liar' should, with the inflexible and merciless Laud, have had it in their power to thrust upon the strongest, wisest, and most religious people of their day the necessity of choosing, either to conform to a ritual which they resented, or to leave the country. Once they had landed in America, the emigrants naturally formed little communities. These were the vital germs of colonies which were presently to take shape and form.

Virginia was the first of the colonies to be established. The name, which is cherished by reason of its own loveliness and its pleasing associations, was originally given to this large and fertile tract of country in honour of Elizabeth, whose vanity was fed by being called the Virgin Queen. Sir Walter Raleigh's name is preserved in the capital of the adjacent colony of North Carolina. For every reason Virginians have a right to be proud of their colony. Its fertile soil and beautiful scenery match its enterprise in every department of wholesome human activity. The novelist has found the achievements of Captain John Smith,

THE COUNTRY AND THE PEOPLE 17

the cruel vigour of Sir Thomas Dale, the erratic reactions of the old chief Powhatan, and the charm of the ill-fated Princess Pocahontas, the kind of material which needs only to be skilfully related to form a story more thrilling than any romance. Chesapeake Bay in those early days was the scene of mingled barbarity and courage, of endurance and of ruthless measures, which perhaps could hardly be avoided, when civilization was struggling for a foothold ; and the fortunes of a continent hung in the balance. Virginia has worthily kept her place in the march of progress ; and Virginians do not hesitate to claim for their colony, not only the merit of age, but the honours of progress also. Happily an Englishman has not to arbitrate, where prejudice and justice so inextricably mingle.

Maryland was the name given to another colony : and this time the name was chosen to gratify the pride or assuage the malice of Charles I, who, no doubt, felt that the glory was partly his, when the colony was called after his wife Maria. Maryland still makes the proud claim to have been 'the first Government in which liberty in matters of faith was established by law.' We should hardly expect so just a claim to have its origin in the firm decision of a devout Roman Catholic, but so it was. Lord Baltimore, whose name was given to the capital, went to America, because as a Catholic, he too, could not worship God in this country according to his conscience. He learnt the lesson of liberty, through being denied it : and resolved that toleration should prevail, where his word was law. He declared, when once he had founded the colony of Maryland, that full liberty was to be given to all. ' No person, within the province,' he said, ' shall be in any ways troubled, molested, or discountenanced for his or her religion, or in the free exercise thereof.'[1] It was a worthy example, and America has at no time turned her back upon it.

The familiar story of the Pilgrim Fathers is woven into the early history of these colonies. It may be that this shining band of heroic souls has received a disproportionate amount of praise: for while their courage was as marked as their sufferings, they were but one little company in a vast crowd, most of whom were unwavering in their resolve to secure liberty of conscience, however high the price they had to pay for it. A nation cannot afford to lose people of this sort. It does not appear that James I or Laud saw any cause for alarm in the departure of these spiritual recalcitrants. Such persons, however, as were capable of appreciating the facts and their significance, could not watch the steady outflow of these resolute men and women, all dedicated to the supreme ideal of liberty, without a sinking of heart. In a dozen years, two hundred emigrant ships had carried twenty thousand from the scene of sharp persecution to a country of spacious freedom.

The Puritans, generally, settled in the territory now known as New England, embracing the four states of Massachusetts, New Hampshire, Connecticut and Rhode Island. Probably, for every reason, they found this region more congenial, with its winter rigours of snow and ice, than the semi-tropical atmosphere of Virginia, and the Southern Colonies. Maine does not appear to have been wholly one at heart, with the religious ideals of New England, and was not admitted to the confederacy of 1643; but though its people were not precisely of the religious

[1] Green, *Short History of the English People*, p. 507.

THE COUNTRY AND THE PEOPLE 19

and political faith of the Puritan colony, they also
' stood manfully by the common cause.'[1]

Charles I graciously bestowed a large portion of the
country on his brother James, the Duke of York ; a
gift which cost the donor nothing, and dignified by
being called after its recipient. The New York State
stretched from the River Hudson to the Inner States.

It was not long, however, before portions of the
large and comparatively populous areas of New York,
were broken off to form the colonies of New Jersey
and Delaware.

The Quakers, with William Penn as their leader,
went further west ; and the wooded country, which
they adopted as their home, was called Pennsylvania.
Georgia was the last of the colonies to be formed,
until after the Revolution which carried with it the
epoch-making Declaration of Independence.

The population of these Colonies consisted at that
time of about 1,200,000 whites, and a quarter of a
million negroes. The numbers may seem trivial to us,
who are accustomed to pack more people into a single
city ; but it should be remembered that England at this
time had a population of not more than five millions.

The faiths held by the groups of immigrants are
indicated by their denominations. They did not
segregate, of course, into little self-contained and exclusive religious communities, occupying isolated areas.
They overlapped and intermingled, but it is possible to
discover certain outlines which indicate the predominance of a particular Church in well-defined areas.

In New England, as we have seen, the religious
complexion was Puritan, and to their honour be it
said, from the very first, the Puritans recognized the

[1] *Encyclopædia Britannica*, XV., p. 301.

value and necessity of education for all the people. It was their noble policy to plant a school wherever there was a group of fifty householders; and where the community numbered a hundred householders they established a Grammar School.

In the Southern Colonies, the Episcopal Church was established by law, and the bulk of the settlers clung to it. Roman Catholics were at home in Maryland. Pennsylvania was, of course, more or less a Quaker State. The Presbyterians and Baptists had their stronghold in New Jersey, while the Lutherans and Moravians from Germany settled in Georgia. The disposition of the religious communities is summarized by Dr. Parkes Cadman as follows: ' The Anglicans were established in Virginia in 1607, the Congregationalists in New England in 1620, the Reformed Church of Holland in New York in 1628, the Presbyterians in Massachusetts in 1629, the Roman Catholics in Maryland in 1632, the Baptists in Rhode Island in 1639, and the Friends in Pennsylvania in 1682.'[1]

This brief review is sufficient to indicate a vast expanse, thinly populated, but containing in all its parts religious communities, which maintained the preaching of the Gospel, and bore their witness to the claims of Christ. The country beyond the Alleghanies was hardly known at all.

The story we have now to tell is of John Wesley's brief sojourn in Georgia, of Whitefield's tireless pilgrimage over a large part of the territory, and then of the definite establishment of Methodist Societies, with their amazing increase and development, so largely due to the devoted and sanctified genius of the indomitable Francis Asbury.

[1] *Wesley as a World Force*, p. 53.

John Wesley.

CHAPTER II

JOHN WESLEY IN AMERICA

' I was like a wandering bird, cast out of the nest, till Mr. John Wesley came to preach his first sermon in Moorfields. O, that was a blessed morning to my soul ! As soon as he got upon the stand, he stroked back his hair, and turned his face towards where I stood, and I thought fixed his eyes upon me. His countenance struck such an awful dread upon me, before I heard him speak, that it made my heart beat like the pendulum of a clock ; and, when he did speak, I thought his whole discourse was aimed at me.'—JOHN NELSON—*Early Methodist Preachers*, Vol. I.

JOHN WESLEY'S brief sojourn in America may seem to have little or no vital relationship to the Methodism of that country. His evangelistic ministry did not begin till after the memorable evening of May 24, 1738. By that time his work in Georgia was at an end, and he had been back in England again for three months. It is no longer possible for us to subscribe to the theory that Wesley was no Christian until the change took place in the little meeting in Aldersgate Street, where, as he says, his ' heart was strangely warmed.' It must be recognized, however, that this experience transformed his whole life and ministry. Before, he had been intensely in earnest : afterwards he was as happy as he was earnest. The bells were set ringing. It was spring-time in his soul. His face shone ; he went about his work with the confident joy of a child of God living in the sunshine of divine favour. It was as though an element had been added to his life which gave another complexion to all he was, and all he did. When he was in America he laboured with the fiery zeal of an apostle, and the hard intensity of a devotee, but he was intolerant, restless, and easily annoyed. His was a nature and temperament that could only be made sweet and attractive by the 'grace of our Lord Jesus Christ.' That work of God had been wrought within him as he left the Aldersgate meeting with heart aflame. He could hardly devote himself with more selfless and unremitting toil to the work of God than he had done in America, but now he went about it with happiness; there was a new song in his mouth. What hitherto had been done from a sense of duty, and that he might save his own soul, was done now in pure gratitude to Christ, who had given him the 'assurance' of salvation. Henceforth he preached that he might save the souls of others. The inflexible High Churchman had become the tolerant and radiant evangelist. He was prepared to follow wherever God led, rather than to mark out his own way, and seek God's blessing upon a self-chosen and restricted programme. What we have to do in this chapter is to give a brief account of Wesley's work in Georgia, and to trace any significance for the continent, that it fairly sustains.

It must be said at once that such significance is slight, compared with the work and influence of other great apostles and evangelists whom we have presently to notice. We may recall, however, that George Whitefield, who landed in Georgia in the same month that Wesley experienced the great change of heart in England, said, 'The good which Wesley has done in America is inexpressible. His name is very precious among the people, and he has laid a foundation that I hope neither men nor devils will ever be able to shake. Oh that I may follow him as he has followed Christ !' Whitefield was a generous soul, and he had reason to love Wesley. It may be, therefore, that such a tribute is rather a proof of his own magnanimity than evidence of Wesley's success.

Wesley saw little to give him satisfaction as he reflected upon his Georgian mission, but we know he was not the kind of man to spare himself. He was more relentless in passing judgement upon his own failures than upon the failures of others. We can see, of course, that he made mistakes; but they were the mistakes of a dedicated soul, and not those of an insincere or indolent man. Not even in the tireless campaign, which he carried on for fifty years in England, was he more in earnest that when he pursued his fretful and feverish ministry in America. What then, it is natural to ask, did he achieve while there, and to what extent can the harvest of his toil be related to the early Methodism of that country ? The answer to such a question must be incomplete. We can only set down the facts as well as we are able, and let them speak for themselves. The Spirit of God often works beneath the surface, and what appears to be a sudden and unrelated revival, is the fruit of toil long since forgotten, and of prayers ' sent up to God ' by an earlier generation.

The way in which Wesley's mind and heart were directed to America is as interesting and remarkable as any chapter in the whole of his long life. It can be briefly told.

His father lay dying. The dear old man's stormy life was at last in haven, and he was resting on the

Saviour's finished work. He found a father's joy in his last days, too, in his sons John and Charles; and it should be acknowledged that Samuel also was his father's comforter to an exceptional degree. The rector had been a painstaking and industrious worker; among his literary productions was a *Commentary on the Book of Job*. He greatly desired that a copy of the book, which was only completed as his own life drew to its close, might be presented to Queen Caroline, and that John should make the presentation. He was too loyal a son not to carry out the father's request. It was, therefore, while John was in London discharging this filial task, that he was first confronted with the needs of America.

It happened in this way; Georgia was the last of the thirteen British colonies to be formed. In 1732 Royal letters patent were issued. The House of Commons granted £10,000, the Bank of England subscribed a similar amount, and General Oglethorpe, aided by friends, raised the figure to a grand total of £36,000 for the requirements of the new Colony, which, with eighteenth-century flattery, was called Georgia in honour of the reigning prince.

General Oglethorpe became the first Governor of the Colony as he deserved to be; for while he was not free from such minor defects as talkativeness and vanity, he was an earnest Christian, and a true lover of helpless humanity. He cared deeply for the unhappy people who had suffered imprisonment from debt, and who found the world cold and inhospitable when they emerged from jail. He laboured to give these, and others who needed help, a new start in life. Accordingly he organized settlements in Georgia for them and their children. In Savannah, in Darien,

JOHN WESLEY IN AMERICA

in Augusta and in St. Simon Island, such settlements were formed. In November, 1732, for example, he had taken out some 116 emigrants. Obviously, to one who cared for the spiritual well-being of the emigrants in their new home, as well as for the re-establishment of their prosperity in the things of this life, there would be a strong desire that they should hear the gospel and be served by some duly appointed minister. Oglethorpe had this concern upon his heart, and the Trustees of Georgia shared his solicitude. The question was, where to find the right man.

Oglethorpe was now in England, anxious to find a clergyman who would go out, and who by his gifts and graces was manifestly the man for the task. The population itself was so unusual as to require a minister of exceptional talent. There were the emigrants of whom we have spoken; there were refugees who had fled from Germany; and then, too, there were the Indians who more than any others were the natives. The latter showed themselves to have the simplicity of children, and with that, a cruelty which was the heritage of savage conditions and centuries of fierce struggle with nature and with man.

The eyes of the Trustees fell upon John Wesley. He was already well known. Dr. Burton, of Corpus Christi College, introduced him to General Oglethorpe, who at once appealed to Wesley to become a missionary to Georgia. To Wesley this was a bolt from the blue, and he was not inclined to agree. He was happy at Oxford; his inclination was to pursue the delights of scholarship, filling his spare time with benevolent work among the needy and desolate. But a love for 'the poor and him that hath no helper,' which had already showed itself among the Oxford Methodists, is an essential quality of the missionary, and one which often evokes the primal missionary enthusiasm. Wesley objected that he had an aged mother, and could not leave her. Susanna Wesley heard of this, and she settled that particular question with the definiteness and courage which might be expected of one who was as richly endowed in intellectual and moral qualities as any woman of her century. 'Had I twenty sons,' she said, 'I should rejoice that they were so employed, though I should never see them more.' The bulwarks suddenly disappeared; and Wesley, left defenceless against the appeal of Georgia, consented to go. He would be, as he significantly and explicitly said, 'A minister to the Colonists, and a missionary to the Indians.' It was like him to be ready almost immediately. On October 21, 1735, he set sail, having as his travelling companions, his brother Charles, Benjamin Ingham, and Charles Delamotte.

The journey across the Atlantic is a familiar story, and one which no student of Wesley's life can afford to ignore. His use of every moment in the improvement of his mind and heart, was characteristic of one whose fierce regard for the sacredness and value of time never forsook him. We know, too, how deeply moved he was, and what anxious questions were raised within him when, during a terrible storm, he saw the Moravians calm in the face of death, and able to sing for very joy while others screamed in terror. The quiet assurance of these godly souls suggested to him that his own spiritual experience was far from being adequate and mature; but he

JOHN WESLEY IN AMERICA

only turned with greater energy, and a more furious zeal to the work which lay before him.

It might be noted, as we dwell upon this part of the story, that Wesley gave many hours a day to the study of German, and the first fruits of this labour was the translation of German hymns. It was Charles Wesley who was to become the greatest of all hymn writers; but the fountain of his rich and joyful song had not yet begun to flow. John, however, though by no means possessed of his brother's inspired opulence, gave the world at this time translations which will not lightly be set aside. We might say of him as Dr. Johnson said of Goldsmith, he touched nothing that he did not adorn. His translations of Tersteegen's 'Thou hidden love of God, whose height,' Richter's 'My soul before Thee prostrate lies,' Freylinghausen's 'O Jesu, Source of calm repose,' and Zinzendorf's 'Jesu, to Thee my heart I bow,' will surely continue to enrich every evangelical hymn book for centuries to come.

It was indeed while Wesley was in America, that he compiled a hymn book, the first of a shining Methodist succession, which bore the title of *The Charlestown Hymn Book*. A study of this compilation shows that thus early Wesley had the admiration for Isaac Watts' hymns which he never lost; one half of the total was by this 'sweet singer of Israel.' Nor did he fail to include Addison's 'When all Thy mercies O my God,' and the noble composition which, perhaps, more perfectly blends devotion, reasoning and poetry than any other hymn in our language, 'The spacious firmament on high.' Thus he taught the people of Georgia to sing hymns of pure merit, and literary excellence. In this respect Wesley gave the Continent a lead which may have had a cleansing and uplifting influence beyond all computation.

Charles Wesley was in Georgia also, but he was no missionary. He had become Oglethorpe's Secretary, and besides being engaged upon town-planning, had quarrelled with the people of Frederica. John journeyed thither to patch up the quarrel, but after eight months, which added little to the lustre of Charles's record, he returned to England, apparently to meditate more upon the wonders of redeeming grace, than to nurse a misery of heart over failure. The music within him was presently to leap forth in hymns of unequalled power and insight. The critics who complain that his song was but theology put into rhyme, are surely lacking in insight. Again and again he rises to the level of poetic grace and beauty, and it is not possible to dream of the day when his choicest songs will be finally discarded.

John Wesley remained in America less than two years. He may have taught much, but he learnt more. A temperament with more than the usual admixture of pride and masterfulness, was daily being chastened. He was learning the hardest of all lessons taught in the school of life. He went to America with a strong sense of self-sufficiency, but he had to acknowledge weakness and failure where others, with motives less exalted, have failed even more egregiously.

The Moravians were a continual challenge to his spiritual standing. When he came into the presence of the German pastors he became aware of a secret and a poise in their lives, to which he was himself a stranger. Spangenburg, one of the pastors, could testify to inward peace and assurance given by the

JOHN WESLEY IN AMERICA

indwelling Spirit. Wesley was perplexed when Spangenburg asked him if he knew that 'Jesus had saved him.' 'I hope He has died to save me,' was the extent of Wesley's testimony. We have only to place this halting confession by the side of the glowing emphasis of his later gospel, to appreciate the inner revolution which took place in Aldersgate Street. Historians have shown a true insight when they have fastened upon the event of May 24, 1738, as an epoch in English history.

It is certain Wesley was never quite happy while in America. How could he be? He had the zeal of a missionary, but that zeal was not fed and sustained by the love which releases the springs of happiness, and invests drudgery with radiant significance. He was obedient to God, but not yet could his rapturous soul exclaim:

> 'My Jesus to know; and to feel His blood flow
> 'Tis life everlasting, 'tis heaven below.'

And so it is, that his sojourn in that country is of more interest for the light it throws upon his own spiritual evolution, than for any significance it had for the people of Georgia.

He soon began to chafe at restrictions which were placed upon his ministry there. He had laid it down with characteristic clearness that he was going to be 'a missionary to the Indians'; and he longed to go among these neglected and ignorant people, and tell them of God: but he found that he was expected to spend most of his time as a conventional clergyman among the immigrants. He was too fiery and too independent to bow meekly to limitations imposed by people who did not share his purposes, nor possess his fine spiritual passion. It was in conditions of this kind he turned, as so many young men have done, for understanding and consolation to a lady who seemed to be a kindred soul. Wesley was always simple and straightforward. He never quite understood the complex and baffling motives of a woman's heart. He confided in Miss Hopkey, and no doubt looked forward to marrying her. She shared his prospect and his hope. The choice was not a wise one, and Wesley had his misgivings. It was of a piece with the frankness of his nature that he should seek counsel of godly men, on a question which most young men decide for themselves first of all, and seek guidance of less enthusiastic persons afterwards. He received no encouragement from those who knew both him and Miss Hopkey. This led to a hesitation which annoyed the lady; and she put an end to his vacillation by marrying another man. The marriage was no doubt a woman's way of avenging herself upon a man who had been weighed in the balances and found wanting.

It would not be worth while to relate this drab and uninspiring story, were it not that it proved an issue which probably changed the course of the world's history. Oglethorpe wished Wesley to marry, in the hope that he would then settle down and prove a more restful and amiable clergyman. What if he had done so? It is vain to speculate; we should then have to envisage an England without a Wesley. What that would have meant for England and the world no one can imagine. The only check to such depressing contemplation is the thought which a faith in God inspires. He is never baffled by man's perversity; and is able to raise up workmen when and how He will.

JOHN WESLEY IN AMERICA

The upshot of the love affair was a piece of high-handed rule on the part of Wesley, and a rather foolish lawsuit on the part of the lady's uncle. Wesley saw that his usefulness and peace of mind were both at an end. He therefore took the advice of his friends, and decided to return to England. He refused to slip away unknown; there was not a vestige of cowardice in his nature. He placarded his intention to leave in the great square of the town that was yet for the most part unbuilt. His own clean cut words are: ' Being now only a prisoner at large in a place where I knew by experience every day would give fresh opportunity to procure evidence of words I never said, and actions I never did, I saw clearly the hour was come for leaving this place; and as soon as evening prayers were over, about eight o'clock, the tide then serving, I shook off the dust of my feet, and left Georgia after having preached the gospel there with much weakness indeed and many infirmities, not as I ought, but as I was able, one year and nearly nine months.'

A few days later, he wrote in his *Journal*, ' I took my leave of America; though if it please God, not for ever.'

For well nigh fifty years he cherished the hope of some day returning, but it was not to be. His work in the three Kingdoms challenged every ounce of his strength and every minute of his time. The fires were lit throughout these islands, and he fed them by ceaseless attention. He travelled continually in all kinds of weather: he preached several times every week; he watched the infant societies, and nursed them into strength and maturity; he guided and directed an organization which often sprang up by an unseen initiative, and took shape without human hands. But it was left for America to be invaded by George Whitefield and Wesley's own disciples. It is the story of these men, their exploits and their devotion we have to consider. The traces of Wesley's immediate and personal impact upon America may be few indeed. He simply touched the fringe of a single colony, and even then did it without much success; but America cherishes the fact of his visit and his ministry with deep gratitude. That great country was not so much his sphere as his school. He went to teach others: he learnt for himself that one vital factor was missing in his spiritual armoury. That factor was found when his soul vibrated with joy on a May evening in 1738, and he went forth with an energy that nothing but death could destroy, and with a gospel that met the needs of all mankind. The world was his parish. When America was attacked by his evangelists, he looked on with prayerful concern; and as wisdom was given to him, he sought to guide, to inspire and to sustain those great and gallant leaders who boldly set out to capture a continent for Christ.

CHAPTER III

WHITEFIELD AND AMERICA

Prepared and ready the altar stands
Waiting the prophet's outstretched hands
And prayer availing, to downward call
The fiery answer in view of all.
Hearts are like wax in the furnace ; who
Shall mould, and shape, and cast them anew ?
Lo by the Merrimac Whitefield stands
In the temple that never was made by hands—
Curtains of azure, and crystal wall,
And dome of the sunshine over all.
                               WHITTIER—*The Preacher.*

THE four missionaries who had gone to Georgia with such confident hope, were now all in England again. While they had been striving more or less successfully with their task, Whitefield had been finding his soul, and laying the foundations in this country, of his almost unequalled popularity as a preacher. The discovery by him of the supreme secret of the new birth had not only furnished him with a gospel which he could preach with rapturous assurance, but it begat within him also a desire to carry the good news to other lands. The resolve to be a missionary grew in firmness, until neither the pleas nor the arguments that he should stay in England could suffice to restrain him. Wesley, we may be sure, was kept well informed while in Georgia, of Whitefield's work at home ; and with the eye, both for a situation and a man, which did so much to create the Methodist Church, he saw that if only Whitefield could be persuaded to assist in the work, Georgia would be greatly enriched. It is true that Whitefield had, for many months, cherished the intention to be a missionary. As early as December, in 1736, when Charles Wesley returned to England, he received a letter from Whitefield ' offering himself to go to Georgia.' A few days later a letter from John Wesley reached him. It was the Wesley we all know who could write in this way. ' Only Mr. Delamotte is with me, till God shall stir up the hearts of some of His servants, who putting their lives in their hands, shall come over and help us when the harvest is so great, and the labourers are few. What if thou art the man, Mr. Whitefield ? '

' Do you ask me,' he writes again, ' what you shall have ? Food to eat, and raiment to put on ; a house to lay your head in, such as your Lord had not, and a Crown of Glory that fadeth not away.'

' Upon reading this my heart leaped within me,' says Whitefield, ' and, as it were, echoed to my call.'

The issue was settled. Whitefield decided, now twenty-two years of age, to be a missionary. He was already famous.

The story of his early life need not detain us. Born at the Bell Inn, Gloucester, 1714, he found his way to Oxford, as a poor lad, and at Pembroke College he acted the humble part of a servitor. He has told the story with a frankness which wins the hearts of all who read it. He wore ' woollen gloves and a patched gown,' and seems to have been so greatly in earnest about the favour of God even then, that he sought to make his poor clothes and ' dirty shoes ' subserve a genuine humility.

While it was to Charles Wesley that Whitefield owed his conversion, he turned to John for spiritual

WHITEFIELD AND AMERICA 35

counsel, for which he never ceased to be grateful. When later, the fires of his soul were lit, he thought of Wesley as his father-in-God, and acknowledged him as his best friend and counsellor.

Whitefield sprang into fame as soon as he began to preach. Not more than once in a century is such a gift bestowed. He was a mere lad when he was seen to possess the secret of the most effective preaching the world had ever heard. It is a poor and pitiful attempt that is often made in these days to rob Whitefield of the crown which his contemporaries so unanimously placed upon his head. His printed sermons may not have the abiding charm and penetration of South, nor the rugged originality and quaintness of Hugh Latimer, but the question is not whether Whitefield could write a great sermon. We may turn over the somewhat faded and jejune pages to-day, and wonder how such sermons as these could have held the crowds in willing bonds, and have made the great men and women of his day acknowledge him as the greatest living master of the pulpit. The answer, of course, is that these sermons as we have them give no adequate idea of Whitefield's preaching. We might as well explore a box of dried grapes to find the purple loveliness of a vineyard. Whitefield himself was a part of his sermon, and a vital part. His voice, his heaven-born eloquence, his intensity and apt appeals; his happy asides, his passionate concern for the souls of his hearers, and his unwavering conviction, all formed a part of that unrivalled equipment.

It is true that while his written sermons do little to disclose the secret of his distinction and power as a preacher, yet the dullest mind must perceive in them his deep piety, his utter subjection to the will of God, and his intense devotion to Christ His Lord and Saviour.

Nothing is more impressive than the number of testimonies which have come down to us from some of the greatest men of his age. Benjamin Franklin, with all his cold, worldly calculation and close-fistedness, had to yield to the entreaty of Whitefield. At first, as he tells us in his autobiography, while listening to Whitefield, he stubbornly resolved to give only coppers, but he gradually yielded, until at the end of the sermon he gladly emptied all his pockets to support the cause for which Whitefield was pleading.

Jonathan Edwards tells the same story, and he was quite another type of man. Mystic and philosopher, with perhaps the keenest mind in America at that time, he simply rejoiced and wept as he listened to Whitefield's glorious torrent of evangelical truth, and entreaty.

It is often said that the tears of the colliers of Kingswood guttered down their grimy faces as they listened to the great evangelist. At the other end of society, the Earl of Huntingdon, and his wife, Sarah Duchess of Marlborough, the Duchess of Queensbury, and the Duchess of Buckingham, alike, confessed that they never heard preaching which searched and exposed their inmost lives as his did.

We shall meet again with the name of Thomas Rankin. Let us quote from him in this connexion. 'The first time,' he says, 'I heard that eminent servant of the Lord Jesus Christ, Mr. George Whitefield, he was preaching his farewell sermon in the Orphan Home Yard in Edinbugh. I had often before had thoughts of hearing him, but so many things had been said to me of him, that I was afraid I should be deceived. I heard him with wonder and surprise, and had such a discovery of the plan of salvation as I had never known before. . . . I remember more of that sermon than of all the sermons I ever had heard, and had a discovery of the unsearchable riches of the grace of God in Christ Jesus, as also how a lost sinner was to come to God and obtain mercy through the Redeemer.'[1] In this tribute we have evidence, not only of Whitefield's power over the heart and conscience of a hard-headed Scotsman, but there is laid bare also the firm and unyielding outlines of his message. He never lost sight, nor did he allow his congregation to lose sight of God's immeasurable grace in Christ, and the way in which a lost soul could find his way back to God.

This man was the precious gift of God to the eighteenth century; and he it was who resolved to set forth for America, caring nothing for the fame and popularity which had been accorded him in unstinted measure.

It happened that he set sail in February, 1738, at the very time Wesley landed at Deal. The vessel which was to bear Whitefield across the Atlantic was still within call, and as soon as Wesley heard of Whitefield's departure he resolved to dissuade him, if possible. It is easy to appreciate the state of mind which led Wesley to take this step. The journey home had given him time to brood over his failure; and he had once more had occasion to witness the quiet confidence of the Moravians, as they faced death itself, and to contrast their peace and assurance with his own fitful uncertainty. He was in no mood at present to contemplate another attack upon Georgia, and he

[1] *Lives of Early Methodist Preachers*, Vol. V., p. 144.

feared that the disappointment which had saddened his own heart would be the lot of all others who set forth on a similar errand. The habit of swift and imperious decision which was to be so characteristic of all his later life, showed itself as soon as he knew of Whitefield's whereabouts. He sent a letter to Whitefield advising him to give up his intention, and remain at home. But Whitefield was not without firm convictions of his own, and in his reply to Wesley he set forth his reasons for proceeding in formal order. ' Firstly, the " enemies of the Lord " would rejoice, and by relinquishing his mission he would give them occasion to blaspheme. Secondly, he had many on board, whose souls were already a sacred charge ; and thirdly, " I see no cause for not going to Georgia." ' [1]

He was to cross the Atlantic thirteen times in all ; but from the day he first left England, his true sphere and home were to be in America ; and while he had neither the vision, nor the constructive statesmanship which gave to Wesley's life and work a distinctive place in the history of the Church of Christ, he must be regarded as a great and successful pioneer. We shall see that he was tireless in his campaigns. He went north and south, never abating a jot in energy or faithfulness, and tens of thousands hung upon his words. He was an evangelist of the new birth : his doctrine of salvation through grace, and salvation to the uttermost, would continually triumph over the Calvinism which he formally approved. Hence he is to be regarded as the pioneer Methodist. When, later, others entered upon a territory, or into any of America's new-born cities, they found often enough,

[1] Tyerman, *Life of George Whitefield*, Vol. I., p. 115.

that one had gone before them, who had prepared their way.

Whitefield was a generous and magnanimous man. He rejoiced in the truth, and was eager in his appreciation of goodness wherever it could be traced. We have seen how firm and instant was his approval of Wesley's work in America. Such a simple and unsought testimony should suffice to restore John Wesley, while in America, to the rank of a true and faithful missionary. His thrilling experience on May 24, 1738, need not stamp upon all his previous life the barrenness of failure.

Whitefield, who was linked with Wesley at the one end, was just as clearly linked with a full and developed Methodism in America at the other. One of his first converts, for instance, Edward Evans, was later to be 'allied with the Methodists' and to receive from their leaders 'permission to preach.' Whitefield was a voluminous letter writer, and equally diligent in keeping a record of his travels and labours. His biographers have never been short of material; but all that we need to do in these pages is to give evidence of his far-spread activities, and remind our readers that wherever he went he went as a herald of the Cross, sparing neither strength of body nor fervour of soul in addressing the vast crowds who everywhere gathered to hear him.

He was, however, not simply a wandering preacher, leaving others to reap where he had sown, he was throughout his life a great-hearted philanthropist. Even in his Oxford days he had collected at least forty pounds a year, to help poor prisoners, and when he left England he took with him the considerable sum of £306 3s. 0d., which he had collected for ' the poor of Georgia.' As soon as he landed he showed a deep concern for the unfortunate, and the needy. There were many who had not found Georgia a land of health and prosperity. Fevers followed hard upon hunger and exposure to such an extent that many parents were cut down, leaving behind them little children for whom there was no sure and adequate provision. For all such, Whitefield's heart was full of tenderness, and his sympathy took the practical form of building an Orphan House. The scheme was not originated by him, for Charles Wesley had cherished the hope of some such institution ; but it was left to Whitefield to give it form and substance. The Oxford Methodists made it a part of their religion from the first, to minister to the sick and needy ; and we know how John Wesley during his long life was always alive to the miseries and privations of his fellow creatures. The forms of social service, which are to-day so commonly regarded as an integral and necessary part of Christian activity, were all anticipated by the Methodist founders ; Whitefield took up the scheme for an Orphan House with eager zeal, and although he had no outstanding gifts as an organizer, he set about the work of building, with an almost fierce earnestness. He returned to England after a brief stay of two or three months, was ordained a priest while at home, and in August of 1739 set forth again for America. In January of 1740, he tells us that he ' chose a tract of land, consisting of 500 acres, situate on the northern part of the Colony, ten miles from Savannah. . . . On the 30th,' so the chronicle continues, ' he took a Surveyor with him and laid out the ground for the Orphan House, which was to be sixty foot long and forty wide. . . . February 4 he

WHITEFIELD AND AMERICA 41

had a meeting with the magistrates and the former trustees of the orphans, when the grant was read over that was given him by the trustees. . . . March 17 he collected seventy pounds sterling. . . . On April 19 he visited Philadelphia, where he preached to upwards of ten thousand people and collected one hundred and ten pounds sterling.'[1] Thus he travelled from town to town, preaching to enormous crowds, and always gathering with unselfish care, as much as the generosity of his hearers yielded, that he might complete the Orphanage, and bring within its shelter the children who were in many instances bitterly in need of the blessings of love and home. The Institution had a chequered career. It flourished while he lived, for he continued to meet its needs with money entrusted to him by friends and admirers during his pilgrimages. When he died, it was left to the care of the Countess of Huntingdon. Two years later, it was burnt to the ground, with only the wings remaining. But though cast down it was not destroyed: the building which now stands upon the same site is the fourth to be erected thereon. A full account of Whitefield's influence on the colonies he visited could only be given by tracing, if it were possible, the result of his philanthropy. The people who learnt of his regard for orphans must have felt a kindling in their hearts for their own unfortunate, and the seeds of a true and Christian social service were sown far and wide.

But Whitefield's name is remembered chiefly because of his preaching. We may wonder how it was that a man of somewhat slender resources should continue

[1] *A Narrative of the Life of the Reverend Mr. George Whitefield*, p. 204.

right up to the day of his death to attract and influence such multitudes. The unsympathetic critic may point out Whitefield's limitations. Lecky, for example, speaks of him as 'chiefly a creature of impulse and emotion,' with very 'little logical skill, no depth or range of knowledge, not much self-restraint.'[1] These withering negatives have an ungracious flavour. Whitefield was more than a clap-trap pulpiteer, and an emotional evangelist : he was an expositor of the gospel, an interpreter of the new birth and the blessings which accompany salvation. Jonathan Edwards did not weep at rhodomontade ; and Benjamin Franklin did not empty his pockets of money which he loved as much as most people, because he had listened to an illogical gospeller. The quickening effect of Whitefield's preaching was universally acknowledged. When he had passed through a town, either in America, in England, or in Scotland, he left behind scores who had become suddenly concerned about their soul's salvation, and a quickened interest on the part of all religious people in the Kingdom of God. Dr. Abel Stevens, the most competent of all Methodist historians in America, says, 'Whitefield journeyed incessantly through the colonies, passing and repassing from Georgia to Maine, like a flame of fire. The Congregationalist Churches of New England, the Presbyterians and the Baptists of the Middle States, and the mixed Colonies of the South, owe their later religious life and energy mostly to the impulse given by his later ministrations.'[2]

Let us glance, by the aid of his own *Narrative*, at his almost incredible industry. In February, 1740,

[1] *Encyclopædia Britannica*, Vol. XXIV., p. 552.
[2] *American Methodism*, p. 30.

WHITEFIELD AND AMERICA 43

he was at Darien. A few days later he was at Savannah again. On April 13 he started off for Pennsylvania, visiting Newcastle and Willingtown. On the 17th he is at Abingdon, and the next day at German's Town. On the 19th he preaches to ten thousand people at Philadelphia. From thence he sets out for New York. On Wednesday, the 23rd, he is at Neshamina, and on the 24th visits Montgomery and Shippack. On the 25th he is at Omwell and the East Jerseys: on the 26th, 27th and 28th he visits New Brunswick, Woodbridge, Elizabeth Town and New York. Three days later he is on the move again: he mentions eighteen other places before, on June 8, he is at Savannah once more.

We have to read this bare record with an imagination which recalls the roads, the slow transport, the ever-changing and varied hospitality. We have also to remind ourselves of the strain imposed by meeting friends, who insist on availing themselves of the warmth of this great man's friendship. Then, greatest wonder of all, ' He preached,' says one of his biographers, ' to ten thousand persons every day for twenty-eight days.'[1] Any one who can read such a chronicle of devoted service with unbowed head, places himself outside the circle of persons endowed with sympathetic intelligence and the grace of appreciation.

The figure of this glorious and prematurely old man, struggling with physical infirmity, travelling unnumbered miles, collecting sums of money for orphans, and above all pleading for souls with unabated intensity, is one which reminds us of the price paid by our fathers for the heritage into which we have entered.

[1] Gledstone, *George Whitefield, M.A., Field Preacher*, p. 5.

Whitefield was an old man at fifty. He not only spent himself with uncalculating prodigality, but he was without either Wesley's tough and wiry constitution, or his discipline and majestic self-restraint. If it were our concern to give a full account of the man, his opinions, and his influence, we should have to take into account his attitude to slavery, and to show that in this respect he failed just where Wesley succeeded so conspicuously. Wesley described slavery as 'that execrable villainy which is the scandal of religion in England, and of human nature.' When Oglethorpe founded the colony of Georgia, he resolved to exclude slavery; and in this he was firmly supported both by the Trustees and the Wesleys; but Whitefield was less resolute. He was indeed a man of his age: he shared the feeling of most of his contemporaries. We might regret he did not meet his contemporary, John Woolman. The slave was not to be ill-treated as a slave; but it was impossible for many of the good men of that day to see how the cotton fields could be cultivated without slave labour, or the negro be entitled to an equal place with the white man. It may surprise us now to read that Gladstone's father was, like many peers and some bishops, a slave-owner, and that when emancipation came he received 'a little over seventy-four thousand pounds for 1609 slaves.'[1]

It would be undiscerning, therefore, if for this reason we reproached Whitefield, since he only held the view shared by many of the great and good men of his day. We might say that he did not rise to the full and obvious height of the gospel argument, that all men are equal in God's sight, and that all should

[1] Morley's *Life of Gladstone*, Vol. I, p. 17.

WHITEFIELD AND AMERICA

be born free. But who of us believes that future generations will not speak with even greater severity of us, when they discuss our Laodicean attitude to war, with its submarines, bombing aeroplanes, and poison gas?

In his will, Whitefield bequeathed the Orphan House, buildings, lands, negroes, books and furniture to 'that elect lady, that mother in Israel, that mirror of true and undefiled religion, the Right Honourable Selina, Countess Dowager of Huntingdon.'[1] One wonders if Whitefield, with all his deep piety, and unaffected humility, did not suffer a loss of spiritual vigour and a degree of healthy independence, through the patronizing friendship, and qualified approbation of so many wealthy people. He remained unspoilt, of course, but the injury sustained through the smiles of wealth is frequently seen in a capricious and fitful sympathy with the poor, and a willingness to underestimate their sufferings. It is a notable fact that Wesley, who was an aristocrat to the finger tips, was far less popular with semi-worldly lords and ladies of high degree than Whitefield. Wesley was too outspoken on the danger of riches to be a favourite in Court circles.

But when all is said, which may tend to reduce the moral and spiritual stature of Whitefield, he remains a grand and colossal figure. England owes to his memory the tribute which gratitude for a passionate evangelism and preaching seldom rivalled, should always inspire: America is his debtor to an even greater degree. He burst the bonds of a narrow Anglicanism, and was the friend of all the Churches. When the Church of England in New York refused to

[1] *Narrative*, p. 251.

lend him her pulpit, he turned without complaining, to the Presbyterians. He quickened hundreds of drooping Churches : the pastors took a new lease of life after listening to his message of God's love : great men paid homage to his power and piety. ' It was wonderful,' says Franklin, ' to see the change soon made in the manners of our inhabitants. From being thoughtless and indifferent about religion, it seemed as if all the world were growing religious, so that one could not walk through Philadelphia in the evening without hearing psalms sung in different families of every street.'[1] No one cared less for popularity. He appears even to have been repelled by praise. His heart during all his working life was torn between England and America. Thirteen journeys in a sailing boat, across the two or three thousand miles which divide the two countries, must have meant that actually over two whole years of his life were spent upon the sea. A sea voyage, however, was not a rest for Whitefield ; he was too well known not to be urged to preach, and too conscientious to shed his sense of responsibility for the souls of all brought under his influence. He worked to the last moment of life. On Friday, September 28, 1770, he preached at Portsmouth, and on the following morning started for Boston by way of Exeter (how generously has America adopted English names !). But the people of Exeter could not let him pass, without urging him to preach ; nor could he refuse their request on the ground of weariness or infirmity, though he might have pleaded both. He had ridden fifteen miles, and was utterly tired, but he braced himself for the occasion. ' Lord Jesus,' he prayed, ' let me go and

[1] Tyerman, *op. cit.*, Vol. I., p. 338.

speak for Thee once more in the field, seal Thy truth, and come home and die.' The prayer was answered. He took his stand on a hogshead, and there under the skies of heaven, the great pioneer of open-air preaching, held forth for nearly two hours to a large congregation. It was the last time that marvellous voice, which so easily compassed a crowd of many thousands, would be heard. He went to bed that night, was attacked once more with the asthma which had helped to break down his strength, and at six o'clock on the morning of September 30, 1770, he passed away. His dust mingles with American soil. When it became known in Georgia, the whole colony went into mourning. Newbury Port, where he was buried, has ever since been a place of pilgrimage. When a few years later Wesley's preachers began to penetrate the vast reaches of the thirteen colonies, they could not fail to see the footprints of one of the greatest of all those ambassadors who have carried the word of the Lord to the perishing souls of men.

CHAPTER IV

THE FIRST SOCIETIES

'I did not think, I did not strive,
The deep peace burnt my me alive ;
The bolted door had broken in,
I knew that I had done with sin.
I knew that Christ had given me birth
To brother all the souls on earth.'
JOHN MASEFIELD—*The Everlasting Mercy.*

THE story of the first Methodist Societies in America, and their formation, introduces us to a group of simple and earnest people. To begin from the first, we need to glance at a rather strange little colony of folks in Ireland. They had come from Germany. Through speaking the German language they had found a difficulty in talking with their neighbours, with a consequent loss in the amenities and quickening influences of the usual spiritual ministrations. The result was a serious declension in piety and morals. They had left Germany because Louis XIV was a fierce persecutor of Protestants, to which faith these sturdy people subscribed. Coming to England at first, by means of English vessels, which Queen Anne had directed to be at their service, some fifty families passed on to Ireland, and then settled in County Limerick. The glow of religion faded, as time went by, and in a few years they were noted rather for their drunkenness and profane language than for religious conviction.

John Wesley heard of these people, and it may be taken for granted that this great evangelist felt that

Embury preaching to the Palatines when leaving Limerick for America, 1760

Record in Embury's pocket-book, Christmas, 1752.

Embury's House in New York.

THE FIRST SOCIETIES 49

strong desire to preach to them, which always became a passion in him when he learnt of people who were neglected, or in deep spiritual need. He tells us in his *Journal* that on June 16, 1756, he rode to Ballingarane, and found there the Palatines. ' They retain,' he says, ' much of the temper and manners of their own country, having no resemblance to those among whom they live. I found much life among the plain, artless, serious people. The whole town came together in the evening and praised God for the consolation.'

Among his hearers was a young man named Philip Embury, though he was not one of the German descendants. There was little to suggest that this resolute, quiet and intelligent carpenter would become famous in two Continents. He had been a Methodist for some three or four years before Wesley preached in his town in 1756, but the visit, and the sermon of Wesley, quickened Embury's zeal, and set him to do such work for God as he was able to do. When a year or two later Wesley visited Ballingarane once more he found a preaching house which Embury had built with his own hands and the help of a few willing friends.

Times were bad, however, and the lure of America was too much for Embury, his wife, and some others; hence a little company sailed for New York in 1760. Among his travelling companions were Paul and Barbara Heck. The names of the others, though for the most part still on record, have little significance for Methodist history. The reason why they left Ireland for America is suggested in some words of John Wesley which not only show us the unhappy lot of the Palatines, but illustrate once more the concern which Wesley always had in his heart for poor people who were in social adversity, or who were the victims of power and wealth. On June 14, 1768, he says in his *Journal*, ' I preached at Ballingarane to the small remains of the poor Palatines. As they could not get food and raiment here, with all their diligence and frugality, part are scattered up and down the Kingdom and part are gone to America. I stand amazed ! Have landlords no common sense (whether they have common humanity or no) that they will suffer such tenants as these to be starved away from home ? '

Embury had been a class leader and a licensed local preacher in Ireland, but to be transplanted in a strange city, in another continent, where there was no spiritual fellowship meant that the fires within him died down, and his Methodist passion for souls was in danger of becoming extinquished. There is no reason to suppose that Embury became an open backslider ; but he was discouraged as he watched some of his fellow-countrymen gradually harden into irreligious ways. He felt no call to preach or to make any sustained effort to maintain his Christian witness. In 1765, however, other Palatines arrived from Ireland and among these were Paul Ruckle and Jacob Heck. It is likely enough that their arrival did something to kindle a spiritual concern in the hearts of those who had preceded them by five years.

The incident which seems to have given definite birth to Methodism in New York is a simple and familiar one. One evening, Barbara Heck, who was sister of Philip Ruckle, went to a house and found her brother with other old friends, playing cards. The solicitude for the souls of the people which had

THE FIRST SOCIETIES 51

been in her heart for years, now suddenly burst into a flame. She seized the cards, flung them into the fire, and repaired at once to the house of Philip Embury in Barrack Street, now Park Place. Her flashing eyes told the story of her spiritual indignation. She was ashamed of the worldliness of her friends. She told Embury that if he did not preach to the people, ' we shall all go to hell together, and God will require our blood at your hands.'

Embury was startled at such a challenge and could only meet it by saying that he had no place in which to preach. But Barbara Heck saw a way; she reminded him that his home might be a house of God, and that he could preach there. Embury consented to preach, and Barbara Heck succeeded in getting a congregation of five persons. These were enrolled as members of a class.

It is natural to pause at this point. Here, in all probability, we have the first Methodist Society formed in America. To-day the Methodists of that Continent number upwards of ten millions in Church membership, to say nothing of the nearly eight millions of children in their Sunday schools and twice the number of adherents. It was from such beginnings as this the mighty Church sprang. Here was the germ cell, a consecrated and earnest woman, a preacher who was a working man and a handful of devout souls who constituted a Methodist Society, and pledged themselves to meet in fellowship and further the work of God.

Before we pursue the story of this little Methodist Society in New York, we ought to devote some attention to another Methodist preacher, who had made his home a base for operations in Maryland. There is no need to decide which should be regarded as holding the claim to priority, Barbara Heck and Philip Embury in New York, or Robert Strawbridge in Maryland. Honours are even. Robert Strawbridge was the type of man who has always held a foremost place in the advance of Methodism. He attracts us at once by his warm piety, his unquenchable zeal and his fearlessness as a pioneer. He, too, was an Irishman, and we are compelled to question if British or American Methodism has adequately acknowledged its debt to the early Methodists of the emerald isle.

We have not far to look in order to find the qualities in Strawbridge which we always associate with the Irish people. He had the same energetic and fiery daring, the same generous and uncalculating readiness to help the unfortunate, and the same indifference to convention and perhaps authority, which we conveniently sum up as ' Irish.' Like the Palatines, he went to America because he believed that there he would find a better livelihood for his wife and young family, and a better future for his own energies. He remained the same fervent evangelist in America that he had been in Drumsnagh, County Leitrim. Plunging into the backwoods he settled, so far as he settled anywhere, in Sam's Creek, Frederick County. He opened his house at once as a place of worship and himself supplied the pulpit. The people were glad to listen to the good news of the gospel, and from the first there was the pulsating quality of a living spiritual community.

It was not long before he built a log-house for a sanctuary in Sam's Creek, and underneath its pulpit he was to lay at rest two of his own little children. The early settlers in America paid a

THE FIRST SOCIETIES 53

heavy price for their adventurous spirit, as such pioneers have always done. It was the little children who fell under the hand of death, where conditions were severe, and doctors far to seek. The eagerness and restless enthusiasm of Strawbridge are seen in his refusal to be satisfied with a single chapel. So dauntless was he in his quest for souls, that he could not even stay to complete the chapel at Sam's Creek. The rude structure, about twenty-two feet square, was never finished. Neither doors nor windows were fitted; he threw prudence and comfort to the winds, and went hither and thither, not throughout his own large county alone, but Eastern Maryland, Delaware and Pennsylvania, preaching with fervour to all who would hear. His neighbours, to their credit be it recorded, admired his life, and furthered his ministry by a compact to care as best they could for his little farm while he was absent on his itineraries. The little society at Sam's Creek consisted at first of about a dozen people; but it was not many years before that society had given four or five preachers to serve as itinerants, and fan the flame which the zeal of Strawbridge had lit. It was he who founded Methodism in Baltimore and Harford Counties. The first native preacher of the Continent is said to have been Richard Owen, who was one of Strawbridge's converts. This devoted man continued for many years as a faithful colleague of Strawbridge, and the two together blazed a trail through wide stretches, founding societies and opening up the way for others who were to follow. If we had space to pursue in detail the work of these two missionaries of the cross, we should have a moving story to tell of happy intimacy and of mutual affection. It was Owen who at last preached the funeral sermon to 'a vast concourse' when Strawbridge died. For the last two years of his life Owen gave himself entirely to the itinerancy. Such men as Watters, Gatch and Garrettson are familiar to students of American Methodism, and these, with others who wrought valiantly, owed their conversion and spiritual instruction to the life-giving ministry of Strawbridge and Owen.

When Strawbridge died the crowds, many of whom had worshipped in the little log house at Sam's Creek, bore him to his grave, 'singing,' says Dr. Abel Stevens, ' as they marched, one of those rapturous lyrics with which Charles Wesley taught the primitive Methodists to triumph over the grave.' The same historian adds : ' He was of medium size, of dark complexion, black hair, had a sweet voice and was an excellent singer. He will be for ever memorable as the contemporary of Embury and Webb in founding the denomination.'

Another fellow worker was Robert Williams. He went out from England to America because he had heard of the needs of that country. He was one of Wesley's preachers ; but whether Wesley sent him or simply acquiesced in his going is not known.

Williams sold his horse to pay his debts, and then set off for his ship, taking as his outfit his saddlebags, a loaf of bread and a bottle of milk. He had not even the money for his passage : but his fellow traveller and friend, Ashton, met the cost of the journey, and the two landed at New York in 1769. Ashton took an active interest in Embury's little charge, but Williams was bent on a bigger task. For six years he gave himself to the work, with its exacting demands. He laboured for a time in New York ; but later

THE FIRST SOCIETIES 55

joined Strawbridge in the founding and development of the work in Baltimore. He had one consuming passion : it was to win souls for his Saviour. He has been called 'the Apostle of Methodism in Virginia.' He it was who formed the first circuit of Virginia. To his ministry we are to look for the influence which led to the conversion of Jesse Lee, a man who was to be a conspicuous figure in many a Methodist Conference, and to win widespread honour because of his ability and consecrated zeal. Williams never rested. North Carolina was for a time his sphere. After a while he, like many others, 'located' as it was called. We shall meet with this term later. When he died in 1775, Francis Asbury was in the neighbourhood, and performed the last solemn offices of burial and preached a funeral sermon. Asbury's sober eulogy ran thus : 'He has been a very useful, laborious man. The Lord gave many souls to his ministry. Perhaps no one in America has been an instrument of awakening so many souls as God has awakened by him.'[1] It is said of Williams that he was 'the first Methodist minister in America that published a book, the first that married, the first that located, and the first that died.'

Since we shall not need to return again to the life and work of Robert Strawbridge, except in an incidental way, this may be the appropriate place to quote a rather stinging observation of Bishop McTyeire which shows, at least, that Strawbridge and Williams did not labour in vain. The first Methodist Conference was held in Philadelphia in 1773, and the Bishop says : 'About one half of the business done besides stationing the ten preachers, was in restraining the

[1] Stevens, *op. cit.*, p. 46.

two grand and impetuous evangelists by whom more than half the work up to date had been performed.'[1] That there was some justification for such a sweeping generalization is seen in the fact that the eleven hundred and sixty members who formed the various Methodist societies at that time, only a hundred and eighty were in New York, and the same number in Philadelphia, while in Maryland and Virginia there were not less than six hundred members.

As soon as we return to New York the name of Captain Webb emerges. There, though the development was slower, the order and stability were the more marked. Captain Webb is one of the picturesque figures of Methodism. He was a man of commanding personality, and a soldier in his courage as in his calling. His life story is a romance, and after his conversion, a record of unremitting labour for God. He was with Wolfe when the heights of Abraham were climbed on the night of September 12, 1759, and there he saw his intrepid leader fall in the hour of victory.

When he was forty-one, Webb heard Wesley preach in Bristol and was there and then converted to God. The following year, 1765, he joined a Methodist Society and was almost immediately licensed to preach. Any one who cares to turn over Wesley's *Journal* will find several references to Captain Webb. It is significant, too, that the word 'fire' is so often used by Wesley when he thinks of Webb. For example, he says: February 2, 1773. 'The Captain is all life and fire: therefore, although he is not deep or regular, yet many who would not hear a better preacher, flock together to hear him. And many are convinced

[1] *New History of Methodism*, II., p. 156.

THE FIRST SOCIETIES 57

under his preaching ; some justified ; a few built up
in love.' It is clear from other tributes to Webb's
preaching, which have survived the years, that even
if his preaching did not reach the high standard upon
which Wesley stamped his unqualified approval, he
had great gifts of natural eloquence. John Adams,
for instance, the second President of the United
States, was often a willing listener, and described
Captain Webb as ' one of the most eloquent men I
ever heard.'

Again, on October 3, 1773, Wesley says, ' I found at
Sarum the fruit of Captain Webb's preaching.' Three
years later he adds : ' Captain Webb kindled a fire
here, and it is not gone out. I endeavoured to avail
myself of the fire which he seldom fails to kindle.'

It is the entrance of Captain Webb upon the scene
at New York which gives him a place in this story.
At the time when the little society was in its struggling
infancy, Webb was the barracks' master at Albany.
One day, when the company of Methodists had
assembled in their place of worship, which was a room
they had rented, they were surprised to see a soldier
enter in full regimentals, and wearing a green shade
over one eye. He walked straight to the front of the
building. It was Captain Webb. The eye shade
covered an orifice which was due to a stray bullet at
the seige of St. Louisberg, in 1745. Whatever flutter
or suspense was caused when these simple people
saw so great a man take a place at the front, they
soon began to rejoice together, for the Captain, by his
testimony and exhortation, disclosed a spiritual joy
and enthusiasm which cheered them all. They
believed he had been sent of God, and his presence
and faithful support were an abiding inspiration at a

time when the fortunes of Methodism might well be said to hang in the balance. It was exactly the quickening influence that was needed. The little society soon experienced the change which transforms a group of people who are chiefly concerned to save their souls, into an aggressive community filled with a passion for the salvation of others. Captain Webb deserves a foremost place in the ranks of those who, by the grace of God, rooted Methodism in New York.

CHAPTER V

PIONEERS

> ' *I go to prove my soul*
> *I see my way as birds their trackless way.*
> *I shall arrive ; what time, what circuit first,*
> *I ask not ; but unless God send His hail*
> *Or blinding fireballs, sleet or stifling snow,*
> *In some time, His good time, I shall arrive ;*
> *He guides me and the bird.   In His good time ! '*
> BROWNING—*Paracelsus.*

NEW YORK has the indefinable quality which gives to the city an almost seductive charm. The Englishman looks first of all at the skyscrapers, and wonders why it should be necessary in a country with areas of such illimitable extent, to pile storey upon storey, until the structures seem almost to pierce the clouds. Nor would a visitor from our country fail to be impressed with the noise and feverish bustle. The trains overhead and underground, the trams grinding round the corners and the fierce, competitive hooting of the ' automobiles ' make conversation in ordinary tones a difficulty.

But the American has reason for his pride in the city. The world has few sights of man's creation more beautiful to offer than New York, silhouetted against the sky from the Atlantic. The eye rests upon a noble picture with deep satisfaction and delight.

It is well nigh incredible that three centuries ago the land upon which New York is built was, for the most part, ' a mass of tangled, frowning forest, fringed with melancholy marshes.'[1] The little collection of huts, which was the first sign of a cultivation superior to that of the dispossessed Indians, was called by their Dutch builders ' New Amsterdam.'

England and Holland were at war at that time, and one of the results of the war was that New Amsterdam passed into the hands of the English. The name was then changed to ' New York.' The choice was dictated by the desire to honour the Duke of York, who was later to be James II. It is one of the ironies of history, that a man so trivial, should have been chosen to stamp his name upon a city so virile and progressive.

The population in 1750 was not more than twelve thousand, which, in another thirty years, had increased to twenty thousand. It is in the heart of this inconsiderable city we have to look for the little Methodist Society, which owed its birth to Barbara Heck and Philip Embury. It should be borne in mind that to no one society, nor to any one specific group of missionaries, must we look for the whole secret of that rapid and amazing expansion of Methodism in America, which is perhaps the greatest miracle of modern Christianity. Methodists were continually coming from Great Britain, who, while they sought an opportunity to obtain a competent livelihood, and provide a home for their children, did not forget to maintain the witness they had borne in the home land. Some of them, no doubt, allowed the fires to die down, but others, hundreds of them, testified for Christ in the locality where they had settled.

Scores of little centres might have been found,

[1] Simon, *John Wesley, the Master Builder*, p. 234.

General Oglethorpe (1698-1785). Captain Thomas Webb.
Barbara Heck (1734-1804).

Richard Boardman and Joseph Pilmoor,
the two volunteers for America at the Conference, Leeds, 1769.

where the leaven was at work, so that when the travelling preachers began to invade the cities and towns, or penetrate the backwoods, they often found a response which gladdened their hearts. They were frequently given the welcome which comes both from eager listeners and old friends.

There was, for example, John King. In 1769 he went from London to America, and is seen, not long after, preaching the Gospel in Philadelphia ' over the graves of the poor in the Potter's Field.'[1] His first pulpit is said to have been ' a blacksmith's block at the intersection of Front and French Streets.' A drunken mob nearly killed him, but he recovered, and continued to preach with ' stentorian voice and excessive ardour.' Others there were who have no memorial, and though their names have now faded from the annals of Methodism, yet by their earnestness and faithful testimony they prepared the way of the Lord, and made many crooked paths straight for the feet of future messengers.

It is, however, to the society in New York that we have to turn, for the most part, for the normal and ordered development which was to result in an organized Methodism. Barbara Heck went one night to the class meeting, and told of a vision she had seen. She had been praying for a more suitable place of worship, and such prayers as hers are never offered in vain. On this particular day she became more than usually conscious of God's nearness. She felt that He was speaking to her. She had the intimacy with God of a true mystic. Presently she was aware, not only of the divine voice, but there appeared before the eyes of her soul, the plan of a

[1] Stevens, *op. cit.*, p. 46.

building in outline and detail. She had no doubt that in such a vision there was the proof that her prayers were answered. So clearly did she see this building of celestial gossamer, that when she told her fellow class members what she had seen and felt, she was able to give an exact account of the plan and proportions of the building. The news was received with joy by all present. They shared her faith; it was the conviction of all that God was about to give them the place of worship for which they had ardently longed, but scarcely dared to expect. But instantly the question was settled in their minds; they were to have a house of God.

Captain Webb took up the proposal with characteristic enthusiasm. He gave thirty pounds of his own money and begged of others. There is a list of names still extant of two hundred and fifty subscribers. The little community was overjoyed as the proposals took shape, and a site was found for the building in John Street. The news reached England, and no one was happier to hear of this development than John Wesley. He sent 'money, books and a clock.' Philip Embury made the pulpit with his own hands. He it was, who, appropriately enough, was chosen to preach the dedicatory sermon. No one can read the journals of the early Methodists without being struck with the fitness and grandeur of the texts they chose for all such occasions. Embury's text was ' Sow to yourselves in righteousness, reap in mercy; break up your fallow ground: for it is time to seek the Lord, till He come and rain righteousness upon you ' (Hosea x. 12).

The custodians of the present John Street Chapel are proud of their history. They claim that this first chapel was built ten years before Wesley's Chapel, City Road. In a recent publication there appears the following description of the old sanctuary. ' The building was of stone, faced with blue plaster, had a sand floor and backless pews ; a fireplace and a high pulpit with brass candlesticks, a slave gallery round three sides, reached by ladders, and the walls were whitewashed. The centre door was used by the white members, the men sitting on the right and the women on the left.'

A minor point for the conscientious historian to settle is, what happened to the clock which Wesley gave, for the same publication says that ' Philip Embury placed the clock in the chapel, which he brought from Ireland in 1760.' It would be pleasant to read an autobiography of Wesley's clock, written in the manner of J. M. Barrie.

It was this early chapel, with its simple architecture and austere accommodation, which may be regarded as the forerunner of the sixty-four thousand Methodist churches and more, which are now studded throughout the United States, many of them of cathedral-like beauty and proportions. If Englishmen experience any wish to claim a share in the building of this first Methodist church in America, they may satisfy their legitimate desire by recalling the fact that when, in 1769, £70 was collected to help in sending missionaries to America, £50 of this was ' appropriated to the payment of the debt on the chapel in New York.'

The community was now growing rapidly, and problems of discipline, of Church order, of an ordained ministry and of some adequate and recognized authority began to emerge. It is often remarked that the fruits of Whitefield's ministry were, to a great extent, dissipated through no organization being created to preserve the precious results of the revivals which so generally attended his powerful preaching. It is the very genius, and to a large extent the secret, of Methodism, that an adequate and appropriate organization came into being as the harvest of Wesley's evangelism was being garnered. The wise and far-seeing men and women of New York recognized that what was needed now was a definite relationship with English Methodism, and especially an oversight and guidance which could only be supplied by men who had had experience of organized church life in the mother country.

Communication between the two countries was a slow and tedious affair in those days, and it does not appear that Wesley and his fellow-workers knew much of what had happened, or was still taking place, in America. But at the Bristol Conference in 1768 considerable light fell upon the needs of America. This was chiefly due to a letter written to Wesley by a layman named Thomas Taylor. Perhaps few documents in the Methodist archives have a better right to be regarded as epoch-making than this long and ably-written letter. Wesley read it to the assembled Conference. A few extracts will indicate its quality. The letter, first of all, gives an account of Whitefield's ministry. 'Divers were savingly converted. . . . Mr. Whitefield's earnestness provoked most of the ministers to a much greater degree of earnestness.' Then follows a simple narrative of Embury's work, which we have already described. Of Captain Webb, he says: 'The novelty of a man preaching in a scarlet coat soon brought greater numbers to hear than the room could contain. But his doctrines were quite

PIONEERS 65

new to the hearers, for he told them point-blank that all their knowledge and profession of religion was not worth a rush, unless their sins were forgiven and they had the witness of God's Spirit with theirs that they were the children of God. This strange doctrine, with some peculiarities in his person, made him soon to be taken notice of, and obliged the little society to look out for a larger house to preach in. They soon found a place that had been built for a rigging house, 60 feet in length and 18 in breadth.' Philip Embury, it seems, had experienced a quickening recently, for, says Taylor, he 'has lately been more zealous than formerly; the consequence of which is that he is more lively in preaching, and his gifts, as well as graces, are much increased.' The story is told also of the way in which, as an undoubted answer to prayer, the society found that a plot of land might be purchased for £600. This was a large sum. They could raise a part, but not the whole, and money could only be borrowed in America at that time at seven per cent. Could English Methodists help? 'Some of our brethren proposed writing to you for a collection in England, but I was averse to this, as I well know our friends there are overburdened already. Yet so far I would earnestly beg: if you would intimate our circumstances to particular persons of ability, perhaps God would open their hearts to assist this infant Society, and contribute to the first preaching house on the original *Methodist* plan in all America.'

The strains of such an appeal are surprisingly modern and familiar; but it is the next paragraph which gives to the letter its significance, in the light of what followed.

'There is another point far more material, and in

which I must importune your assistance, not only in my own name, but in the name of the whole Society. We want an able, experienced preacher; one who has both gifts and graces necessary for the work. God has not despised the day of small things. There is a real work in many hearts by the preaching of Mr. Webb and Mr. Embury; but although they are both useful, and their hearts in the work, they want many qualifications necessary for such an undertaking where they have none to direct them. And the progress of the Gospel here depends much on the qualifications of the preachers.

'I have thought of Mr. Helton, for if possible, we must have a man of wisdom, of sound faith and a good disciplinarian; one whose heart and soul are in the work, and I doubt not, but by the goodness of God, such a flame would be soon kindled, as would never stop until it reached the great South Sea. We may make shifts to evade temporal inconveniences, but we cannot *purchase* such a preacher as I have described. Dear Sir, I entreat you, for the good of thousands, to use your utmost endeavour to send one.... With respect to the money for payment of a preacher's passage over, if they could not procure it, we would sell our coats and shirts to pay it. I most earnestly beg an interest in your prayers, and trust you and many of your brethren will not forget the Church in this wilderness.'

The appeal, with its pathetic trust, both in the willingness and ability of Wesley to send a preacher, could not lightly be dismissed. Wesley was not able to comply with the request at the Conference of 1768, but he could not, even if he wished to do so, dismiss America from his mind. He began to collect money

The First Methodist Church in America, John Street, New York, 1768.
The Rigging Loft which preceded John Street Church to-day,
  the Church.

PIONEERS

for the needy and heroic little band, and directed that, here and there, a copy of Taylor's letter should be read. During the same year Wesley met Whitefield, who was in this country for the last time. Wesley enjoyed the benignant and brotherly intercourse of his prematurely old friend, and saw clearly enough that Whitefield's bodily strength had reached the breaking point. ' His soul seemed to be vigorous, but his body was sinking apace.' We cannot believe that these two men should spend much time together before the needs of America became a topic of conversation. Whitefield could supply fact and detail which would give point to the earnest appeal of Taylor.

The Conference of 1769 met in Leeds, and, tempted as we may be to dwell upon the subject which first of all occupied the thought of those gathered together under Wesley's Presidency, we have to remember that this is not our subject. Suffice it to say that Wesley, there and then, dealt in characteristic way with those who criticized his actions and his influence. He outlined such arrangements as seemed good to him, and his loyal sons, for the existence of an organized Methodism after his death, and then passed on to consider America.

The Minutes of Conference for that year contain the following stiff and formal entry :—

Q. 13. We have a pressing call from our brethren in New York (who have built a preaching house) to come over and help them. Who is willing to go ?
A. Richard Boardman and Joseph Pilmoor.
Q. 14. What can we do further in token of our brotherly love ?

68   DAWN OF AMERICAN METHODISM

A.   Let us now make a collection among ourselves.

This was immediately done, and out of it £50, as we have seen, was allotted towards the payment of their debt, while the remaining £20 was given ' to our brethren for their passage.'

Thus the Methodist Conference in England, by the commission of two of its preachers, was linked in living union with the Methodism across the Atlantic. The two men so appointed were admirably chosen, and possessed the gifts and graces which Taylor described as necessary.

Boardman was thirty-one years of age. He was still in the shadow of a great bereavement, for he had just buried his wife and little daughter. Pilmoor was about the same age. He had been converted under the preaching of Wesley and placed by him at the Kingswood School. His portrait indicates that he deserved the tribute of being a man ' of fine presence, much executive skill, easy address and rare courage.'

The decision of the Conference to send these two men to America was a subject of stupid mirth and ridicule in the newspapers. Whitefield was described as ' the Archbishop of Boston,' and Wesley, for some inscrutable reason, was ' the Archbishop of Pennsylvania.' Poor Dr. Dodd, who was soon to expiate his crime of forgery upon the gallows, was said to be a candidate for Methodist honours ! This serves to remind us that Methodist people were not always popular, and Wesley had more shafts of ridicule directed against him than we generally appreciate.

It was enough, however, for the two missionaries to have been thus designated. In a short time they

PIONEERS   69

were on their way, and after a nine weeks' voyage they landed on October 20, 1769, at Gloucester Point, New Jersey. It was but a short journey of five miles up the Delaware River to Philadelphia, where Captain Webb was ready to receive them with unaffected joy.

Boardman soon set off on his journey of eighty-five miles for New York, while Pilmoor remained to carry on the work at Philadelphia. Methodism, with all its readiness to carry the gospel to the people of the villages and the backwoods, was quick to seize upon the strategic points, and the first two missionaries made the two largest cities of the States the centre of their operations. Pilmoor was thrilled with the response given to his ministry. The young people drew around him with affectionate loyalty. Crowds gathered to hear the gospel from his lips.

Boardman found the same spirit of hearing at New York. The two brethren exchanged stations every few months, and in this way promoted the catholicity which marks a living Church.

It was a means of refreshing to their own minds and souls also, to exchange responsibilities. Both of them, however, seized every occasion to preach the gospel elsewhere. They had not come with a supine content if they but ' held their own,' nor would it satisfy them to build up a single, strong Church. Boardman, we are told, ' made missionary journeys from Philadelphia into Maryland, and preached in Baltimore. Pilmoor visited Captain Webb on Long Island and journeyed along the Sound to New Rochelle, where later was formed, though not by him, the third Society in New York State.'[1]

Philip Embury was released from the care of the

[1] *New History of Methodism*, II., p. 66.

New York Society with the arrival of Boardman, but he did not make this an excuse for slackening his labours. With a few others, mostly old friends, he founded another Society at Ashgrove, a small town about a hundred and fifty miles from New York. There he continued, a faithful witness and an earnest local preacher, until 1775, when he died as the result of an accident. A glimpse, both of Boardman's successful labours in New York and of his own personal joy, is seen in the following extract from a letter of his to Wesley: ' Our house contains about seventeen hundred people. About a third part of those who attend are glad to get in, the rest are glad to hear without. There appears to be such a willingness in the Americans to hear the word as I never saw before. They have no preaching in some parts of the back settlements. I doubt not but an effectual door will be opened among them. O! may the Most High now give His Son the heathen for His inheritance. The number of blacks that attend the preaching affects me much.'[1]

In the summer of 1770 Pilmoor went to Baltimore and other parts of Maryland, and found occasion to join hands and heart with Strawbridge, Owen, King, and Williams. The two centres of Methodism with all their developments, which are represented on the one hand in Embury, Barbara Heck and Captain Webb in New York, and in Robert Strawbridge and his fellow workers in Maryland on the other, were now no longer separate fields of toil. The brethren met and rejoiced together, and Methodism was as truly one outwardly, as in the Spirit which gave birth to its far-reaching activities. What if this unity had

[1] Stevens, *op. cit.*, p. 51.

never been broken ! It is interesting, too, to know that, just as Whitefield had called on the Methodist missionaries at Philadelphia a few weeks before his death, when he was taking the last of his long and exacting pilgrimages from Georgia to New York, so Pilmoor preached his way through Virginia, the Carolinas and right through to Savannah. There he paid a visit to Whitefield's Orphan House. The journey took him nearly a year, and the world is the loser through no record existing of his hairbreadth escapes and innumerable thrilling experiences. We would gladly surrender many a modern volume to have the story of Pilmoor's pioneer journey through such fascinating country.

America was ready for further developments. Wesley had sent two of his preachers, but the need was greater than ever. The very success of Boardman and Pilmoor intensified the need they were sent to supply. Little jets of light could be seen shooting up from New York to Georgia. These precious little societies needed careful nursing and guidance. It was a moment which provided an unprecedented opportunity. Would the Methodist people of England still further consider the claims of America ? Captain Webb had returned. He could, and did tell the story of societies springing up in nearly every town, and of vast districts where, above all else, men, women and children needed and desired the gospel. Wesley might be thought to have enough on hand without America. His wife had just left him in another fit of madness, and although he said with apparent severity, '*Non eam reliqui* : *non dimisi, non revocabo,*' he must have suffered the anguish of a lonely and humiliated man. He had also just preached the funeral sermon for his old companion and former colleague, Whitefield, who had remained faithful in his affection for Wesley, in spite of the Calvinism which threatened to divorce him completely from Wesley's list of dear friends. The Countess of Huntingdon was making mischief at Trevecca, and had to be dealt with by the sharp pen of Fletcher, whose saintliness only added force and verve to his theological arguments. Wesley himself was now sixty-eight years of age ; but. he knew nothing of the weariness which makes men delegate their duty. At the Conference of 1771 the question was asked with simple directness : ' Who will go to America ? ' Five persons offered to go. Two were chosen. One of these was Richard Wright. It was, perhaps, an unfortunate choice, for Wright was lacking in moral fibre and constancy, and in two years it was clear to all careful observers that his place was not in the ranks of American missionaries. He returned to England, and in 1774, was appointed as an itinerant preacher in this country. After another three years he disappears from the records, and was speedily forgotten.

But the name of the other missionary quickens the pulse even to hear it repeated. It was *Francis Asbury*. He will dominate this story now for many a long year. Of all the gifts which England may have bestowed on America it may be said by those who know best, that the greatest of all was the gift of Francis Asbury.

CHAPTER VI

FRANCIS ASBURY AND THOMAS RANKIN

'*I am always on the wing but it is for God.*'—FRANCIS ASBURY.
'*If my brethren who first came over had been more attentive to our discipline, there would have been, by this time, a more glorious work in many places of this continent.*'—THOMAS RANKIN.

FRANCIS ASBURY was twenty-six years of age when he embarked, with the blessing of Wesley and the Conference of 1771, for America. The story of his early life is almost without incident. Born in 1745 near Hamstead Bridge, in Staffordshire, his parents were intelligent working people; and from this sturdy stock Asbury inherited the toughness of physical fibre, and the rich common sense which served him so efficiently for the forty-five years of his ministry in America. His parents found their spiritual needs met by the ministry of the Anglican Church, but Francis was deeply interested in the Methodists while still a boy, and at sixteen years of age was truly converted to God.

John Wesley discovered the lad, as he so often discovered young men with gifts and graces, and sent him to supply for an itinerant preacher who had broken down in the Staffordshire and Gloucester area.

The picture we have of him at this time is that of a young man, serious in his deportment, almost prematurely wise, and greatly devoted to books. He had not the advantage of a good education, but his strength of mind and devotion to learning possibly did more to make him a competent leader in the kind of enterprise that lay before him, than even a university education could have done. It might be said that his hunger for books was life-long. He never lost his love for the study of Greek, Latin, and Hebrew; and though in these subjects, as in other branches of study, he was self-taught, so thorough and systematic were his habits, that he gained a command of these languages which enabled him to read them with a fair degree of ease; and during his long life they never ceased to fascinate and instruct.

His temperament was tinged with a sombre hue, and at times he was almost melancholy. This was due in part to the fact that he hardly ever seems to have enjoyed vigorous health. His voluminous *Journal* attest his physical discomforts and minor ailments. He frequently complains of fevers, of a sore and ulcerated throat; gastric trouble of some sort joined to these, seems to have subdued his spirits, and to have added greatly to his hardships.

It was at the Bristol Conference in 1771 that he offered to go to America. No one present then, we may be sure, had any idea of the epoch which such an offer created. It was a turning point in the history of a continent. Who would have thought that this obscure itinerant, with the habits and limitations of a country breeding, was to become the same great evangelist, pioneer and organizer in America that Wesley had proved himself to be in England? It is fair to Wesley, however, to say that he must have had a high opinion of Asbury's sterling merits, since

Site of Asbury's Birthplace.

Home of Asbury's Childhood—endmost house on left.
(Newton Road, Great Barr.)

FRANCIS ASBURY & THOMAS RANKIN 75

only a year later he appointed him 'assistant or superintendent of the American societies, though he was but twenty-seven years of age.'[1]

Asbury and Richard Wright sailed together. The parting between Asbury and his parents seems to have given the acutest distress both to himself and to them. The father and mother felt that they might never see him again ; nor did they. Though forty-five years of unremitting toil lay between him and the end, he never returned to England : he gave his heart as well as his years to America. The societies were as children to him, and he could not bear to leave them.

He is described by one historian as having 'a mind with an eminently military cast.' The truth of this is seen in his immediate insistence upon a severer discipline among the members of the societies. He was inherently a man of method and of order. Nothing slipshod was ever tolerated by him. The neatness of his dress always testified to his love of what was seemly. Beneath the gentle features of the youthful leader there was a resoluteness which could command and secure obedience.

He was not wholly without a sense of humour ; many a sly hint in his *Journal* shows that he had grace to enjoy the fun of life, and see the weaknesses and the whims of other people. But the impress of his passion for doing things decently and in order was stamped upon all the societies he visited.

He protested also in his own quiet and effective way against the tendency of preachers who were so fond of life's amenities that they inclined to settle down in a comfortable pastorate. Asbury never settled down.

[1] Stevens, *op. cit.*, p. 61.

He was, as he says, 'always on the wing, but it is for God.'

'I am dissatisfied,' he says; 'I judge we are to be shut up in the cities this winter. My brethren seem unwilling to leave the cities, but I think I shall show them the way.' And he did so, both in precept and example.

It is said that he rode more than two hundred and seventy-five thousand miles, and most of them on horseback. When we face the prosaic fact that this figure represents an annual pilgrimage of over six thousand miles; or if we pursue the simple arithmetic, an *average* of over one hundred miles every week, we can understand that indeed he was 'always on the wing,' and that he would have little patience with the preachers who made a comfortable nest for themselves in a city manse. 'My way,' he says, 'is to go straight forward and aim at what is right. I must mind my own business, which is enough for me.' But it was his business to see that others did not stagnate or turn a deaf ear to appeals that came from the vast stretches, where a thin population was without spiritual ministrations of any kind. Dr. Stevens in his *American Methodism* makes a bold claim for Asbury, which the facts go far to sustain, when he says, 'Neither Wesley nor Whitefield laboured as energetically as this obscure man. He exceeded them in his annual travels, the frequency of his sermons and the hardship of his daily life.'[1]

The secret of his unrivalled influence and power was rooted in his simple dependence upon God. He might be said to have prayed almost without ceasing. He resolved, early in life, to pray ten minutes

[1] p. 109.

in each hour. He never entered and left a home without praying. Prayer was to him a necessity of every waking hour. He rejoiced in the Lord's favour, and sought it as the sunshine of his soul. It was his trust in God which freed him from all fear of danger. Neither sickness nor death could terrify him. The hardships he endured were of almost every kind. He was misrepresented and driven into hiding. He had colleagues who sometimes did not understand him and frequently underestimated his intellectual and moral reserves. Both his work and his methods were at times treated almost with contempt. He was exposed to cold and rain. He frequently had only the meanest shelter and the coarsest food. 'The house in which we live,' he writes, while on one of his journeys, ' is not the most agreeable ; the size of it is twenty feet by sixteen and there are seven beds, and sixteen persons therein, and some noisy children. So I dwell amongst briars and thorns ; but my soul is in peace.' At another time he writes : 'I have escaped from filth, fleas and rattlesnakes.' It was a typical incident, when he rode a dozen or fifteen miles, and it was so cold that the water froze from his horse's nostrils. The journey was with no other object than to preach to a mere handful of people. But he never asked for large congregations ; he would preach wherever two or three were gathered together. ' He preached mostly in private houses,' says Dr. Stevens, ' sometimes in court-houses, less frequently in churches, sometimes in the woods, at others in prisons, especially where there were culprits condemned to death : and that was a day of much hanging. Sometimes he mounted a waggon at the gallows, impressing with awe the hardened multitude.' This was the kind of man who was sent to take up the work and assist the brethren Pilmoor and Boardman. They were a happy trio : they planned their work upon a large scale. If ever men had reason to ask ' What are these among so many ? ' it was these three. The work spread like wild fire : everywhere there was a response to the Gospel. Preachers emerged from the Societies with at least the supreme qualification of a knowledge of sins forgiven, and a burning zeal to tell others the story of redeeming love. The three brethren agreed for the first half of 1772 that Boardman should enter New England, that Pilmoor should attack the South, and that Asbury should make Philadelphia the centre of his living ministry.

In Baltimore, a little later, Asbury arranged a circuit of two hundred miles, with twenty-four appointments, which were covered by him every three weeks.

It was manifest, however, that more workers were needed : and good Captain Webb felt that Wesley should send out some older men, with more experience and the wisdom which is supposed to come with years. Hence, he started off for England to lay the case before Wesley ; and it was largely in reply to such an appeal that Wesley sent two other men. The appointment of one of these only just escaped being a tragedy. The two newly appointed preachers were George Shadford and Thomas Rankin. The letter which Wesley addressed to Shadford, who was a happy and most lovable man, is a gem :

' Dear George,

The time is arrived for you to embark for America. You must go down to Bristol, where you will meet with T. Rankin, Captain Webb

FRANCIS ASBURY & THOMAS RANKIN 79

and his wife. I let you loose, George, on the great Continent of America. Publish your message in the open face of the sun and do all the good you can.

I am, dear George,

Yours affectionately,

JOHN WESLEY.'

Thomas Rankin, who was sent to take over the superintendency from Asbury, demands a fuller notice. He has a place among those whose records are found in *Early Methodist Preachers*. In volume five of that series there is the story of his life ' written by himself.'

A Scotch lad, he heard George Whitefield preach in Edinburgh, as we have seen.[1] He was converted, and soon after availed himself of an opportunity to visit South Carolina, on a business errand for a relative. There he saw enough to distress his soul. Rum was cheap and ' I observed a very great profligacy of manners among the poor blacks, whether they were free or slaves.' The first time he saw Wesley is worth recording in his own words. He had been home some months, and though Wesley had often preached in Scotland, Rankin always just missed hearing him. It was not until he came as far south as Sunderland that the joyful occasion occurred, and even then he arrived too late to hear the sermon. ' When we came to Morpeth, we found he had preached at twelve instead of one o'clock. We put up our horses and hastened to the marketplace, where he was giving out the last hymn. We were not too late,

[1] p. 36.

however, for the Divine blessing. As soon as I came near to hear the words of the hymn, I was so struck with the presence of God, that if I had not leaned on a friend's arm, I should have fallen to the ground. The words of the hymn were :—

> Now, even now, the Saviour stands,
> All day long He spreads His hands.

'It was now that the foundation of that union was laid, which remained inviolate for thirty-one years, to the time he (Wesley) was called to his great and eternal reward.'[1]

Rankin soon became one of Wesley's itinerants, and after appointments in Devon and Cornwall, Epworth and London, he set forth as Wesley's travelling companion in 1770. Wesley must have known his man : and he judged Rankin to be the kind of person America needed.

It is not so clear to us now that the appointment was a wise one. Asbury had commended himself to his brethren, and it did not seem necessary that he should be called upon to resign his authority to Rankin. He did so, however, without a murmur, in June, 1773. The qualifications for such a leadership, without which all others were in vain, were a good temper, a cheerful disposition and fortitude when disappointments came. These Rankin does not seem to have possessed. He expected more than he found : the weakness of some of the societies chagrined him ; and he showed his feelings in a way which helped nobody. Rankin was an earnest and devout man : his love for Christ and the brethren breaks out continually in expressions of rapture ; but he was not

[1] *Early Methodist Preachers*, Vol. V., p. 166.

the man to press steadily on in a day of small things, and secure the order he desired by constant and persuasive methods. He evidently did not know how great a man was Asbury; and it may be doubted if Wesley knew either, when he appointed Rankin to supersede him. There is no need that we should determine which was the more to blame, Asbury or Rankin: perhaps blame falls lightly on both when all the facts are known, but it is evident that they were not the two men to run happily in double harness. Rankin was blunt, inconsiderate and unsympathetic; Asbury kept his counsel but disapproved of much that Rankin said and did. 'From what I see and hear,' Rankin said with almost brutal frankness, ' and so far as I can judge, if my brethren who first came over had been more attentive to our discipline, there would have been by this time a more glorious work in many places of this Continent.'

If we knew nothing more than the few facts which relate to Rankin's relationship with American Methodism we might assume that he was an uncongenial colleague, and without the stuff of which pioneers are made. He complained that ' the amount of all members of the different societies did not exceed one thousand one hundred and sixty.' This was surely no small achievement when all the facts are considered; but Rankin appears to have been in rather a poor temper most of the time, and especially during the early months of his stay in America. It hurt Asbury to hear the work belittled by the man who had been placed in authority. The relations were often strained between these two good men, and Wesley came to hear of it. He did what seemed to him the right thing, and requested that Asbury should return to England. Happily at the time the peremptory letter reached Rankin, Asbury was many miles away, pursuing the task which Rankin had assigned him in Norfolk, Virginia. Asbury did not want to go to this station ; but we can see now that the over-ruling providence, which again and again intervened in the history of this great movement, saved Asbury for America, and by doing so secured for that country the greatest evangelist, leader and statesman whom Methodism had in her ranks.

We must avoid, however, magnifying the importance of these details. Rankin and Asbury were both good men and true, and both cared supremely for the societies which they helped to bring into being and to nourish. They had many happy moments together, and both were big enough not to nourish petty jealousies, or let the work of God be injured by personal considerations.

An event of great importance was the first Methodist Conference to be held, over which Rankin presided. Ten brethren in all met at Philadelphia on Wednesday, July 14, 1773, and remained in session until the Friday. The names of most of the preachers are fairly well known to us. They are Thomas Rankin, Joseph Pilmoor, Richard Boardman, Francis Asbury, Richard Wright, George Shadford, Thomas Webb, John King, Abraham Whitworth and Joseph Yearbry.

The question which above all others called for serious consideration was the introduction of classes, similar to those which meant so much to English Methodism, and the discipline which only could be obtained by their existence. The American preachers did not favour these society classes, but both Rankin and Asbury were adamant. They saw that here was

FRANCIS ASBURY & THOMAS RANKIN 83

a question which was vital. The 'Minutes' of the Conference show how fundamental were the decisions arrived at:

> 1. Ought not the authority of Mr. Wesley and that Conference to extend to the preachers and people in America, as well as in Great Britain and Ireland? *Answer:* Yes.
>
> 2. Ought not the doctrine and discipline of the Methodists as contained in the Minutes to be the sole rule of our conduct, who labour in the connexion with Mr. Wesley in America? *Answer:* Yes.
>
> 3. If so, does it not follow that if any preachers deviate from the Minutes we can have no fellowship with them till they change their conduct? *Answer:* Yes.

There was no uncertain sound: the first Conference had justified itself. A slackening of order, where elements of rude strength abounded, would have resulted in disorder and ultimately in chaos. Methodism was saved by the wisdom and firmness of those who by the providence of God were its leaders. It was Rankin and his dour steadfastness, and Asbury with his unyielding loyalty to Methodist principles who combined at this critical moment to lay down the firm foundations upon which the stately structure of the Methodist Church in America has ever since reposed.

The Conference went on to lay down certain rules for the Preachers, which have some relevance to events of great importance in future days:

'Every Preacher who acts in connexion with Mr.

84 DAWN OF AMERICAN METHODISM

Wesley and the brethren who labour in America is strictly to avoid adminstering the ordinances of baptism and the Lord's Supper.'[1]

That is by no means the last we shall hear of this question. Nor was it meaningless, as we shall see, that the Rule relating to the Lord's Supper should be particularly urged in Maryland and Virginia. This was the territory where the fearless and unconventional Strawbridge had laboured, with his devoted colleagues.

The Conference told Robert Williams that he might sell the books he had already printed, but he was to print no more, nor were any of the preachers to reprint any of Mr. Wesley's books, 'without his authority (when it can be gotten) and the consent of their brethren.' Finally, 'Every preacher who acts as an assistant to send an account of the work once in six months to the General Assistant.'

Boardman and Pilmoor returned to England soon after this Conference. They had seen that trouble with England was in the offing. 'When they saw the terrible certainty of war they quietly retired, embarking together for England on Sunday, the 2nd of January, 1774, after commending the Americans to God. They left 2073 members in the Societies, ten regularly organized circuits and seventeen preachers.'[2]

Richard Wright also returned early in 1774. Captain Webb stayed for a year after Boardman and Pilmoor left, doing all he could to increase and safeguard the work of God. He, too, a little later returned to England. He gave nine years to American Methodism and then returned to Bristol. He died suddenly, on

[1] *New History of Methodism*, Vol. II.
[2] Stevens, *op. cit.*, p. 71.

FRANCIS ASBURY & THOMAS RANKIN 85

December 1, 1796, and his body was laid to rest in Portland Chapel, Bristol. The mourning crowds attested his great qualities. America owes much to Webb, who distinguished himself even more as a soldier of Christ, than as a soldier of his King.

The war drew near, with the Revolution, and the ultimate declaration of American Independence. We shall see what trying days lay ahead of the numerous and scattered Methodist Societies.

CHAPTER VII

THE REVOLUTION

' Methinks I see in my mind a noble and puissant nation rousing herself like a strong man after sleep, and shaking her invincible locks. Methinks I see her as an eagle mewing her mighty youth, and kindling her undazzled eyes at the full mid-day beam, purging and unscaling her long abused sight at the fountain itself of heavenly radiance, while the whole noise of timorous and flocking birds, with those also that love the twilight, flutter about, amazed at what she means.'—MILTON—*Areopagitica.*

THE struggle which was now pending between America and England almost shattered the Methodist organization, which had begun to assume an appearance of permanence and progress. There is no need that we should tell once more, in any detail, the tragic story of England's blunders in dealing with America, with all their far-reaching consequences. Every one knows how perverse and obstinate was George the Third. It is no source of pride, to so great a nation, to recall that this poor, little recalcitrant man, should, by the accident of birth have been placed where he could summon to his side the lethargic Lord North, and pursue a disastrous policy, in spite of such counsellors as Pitt, Burke and many another wise man. It was the very year (1760) when Philip Embury and his companions landed in New York, that the Government resolved upon the taxation of America. It may be argued, of course, that England had some right to expect help from the Colonies; but no one who knew

1. Dr. Coke's Birthplace at Brecon.   2. Thomas Coke, LL.D.
3. No. 6 Dighton Street, Bristol, the house in which Dr. Coke was set apart as General Superintendent for America.

the type of man America had bred, could suppose that England would succeed in levying taxes on these growing Colonies, without first of all coming to some agreement with their representatives. England attempted to treat a race of strong men as though they were children; and the consequences are known to all. The rumblings which foretold war, might have been heard for many years, but the King was deaf to them all. Any set of men who can establish the proposition that they are taxed, without having any part in saying to what extent, and for what reason they shall be taxed, have a just cause for protest. The American farmers and backwoodsmen might be slow to think and act; but when once a conviction had been formed in their minds, they were resolute in acting upon it. In many cases they were the second and third generation, born in a country where life was, for many of them, a daily struggle with thorns and briars, with bogs and forest, with wild animals and wilder men. It could hardly be expected therefore that they would readily kindle into a flame of devotion to a country from which their forefathers had in so many cases fled at the stern dictates of conscience.

Burke's description of them will come to the mind of all familiar with his mighty speeches. 'Religion,' he says, 'always a principle of energy, in this new people is no way worn out or impaired: and their mode of professing it is also one main cause of this free spirit. The people are Protestants, and of that kind which is the most adverse to all implicit submission of mind and opinion. . . . All Protestantism, even the most cold and passive, is a sort of dissent. But the religion most prevalent in our northern

Colonies is a refinement on the principle of resistance : it is the dissidence of dissent, and the protestantism of the Protestant religion.'[1]

James Otis, who has been called 'the morning star of the Revolution,' voiced the anger of the people, and foretold disaster. But such protests as his were dismissed with ridicule. The Government replied by passing the preposterous Stamp Act. The anger of America at this was violent, and Massachusetts was the first of the Colonies to make a direct appeal to war as the only tribunal which remained. England could do nothing that was generous or wise. It was clear that the taxes could not stand ; but instead of repealing the whole, the narrow and purblind King, with Lord North, insisted on retaining the tax on tea ! They did so, not because of the financial gain, but for the sake of what they called principle. Burke, Chatham and Fox opposed the King's policy, but they were unavailing. The end of it all was a war, which humiliated England, tore from her Empire the thirteen Colonies, and gave birth to the American nation. We may say that it is better so : but the manner of its accomplishment was a tragedy.

The effect of the war upon almost all the missionaries from England was that they returned home. They were not cowards. To withdraw was probably best for the Christian communities themselves, as well as for future enterprise. England was hated furiously, and especially so when the sons of America, under the magnificent leadership of Washington, fell in war, and when the whole army sometimes suffered grave defeat. The missionaries therefore were suspect as well they might be ; for not even the folly of the

[1] Speech on Conciliation with the Colonies.

THE REVOLUTION

Government could quench the love of their own country which glowed within their breasts. Every Englishman might easily be a storm centre. Let it once be known that a community of Christian people had for their pastor, a man who owned allegiance to England, and all its members would be at once the objects of dislike and even persecution. We have therefore to envisage America at this moment as largely bereft of the Church leaders, whose piety, learning and guidance had helped to develop the powerful or nascent Churches throughout the Colonies.

We have seen that Boardman and Pilmoor returned before the war broke out. Thomas Rankin was perhaps not loathe to leave a country, where he did not easily fall into the ways of the people, nor readily conceive an affection for those to whom he was expected to minister. He says, ' In the beginning of June, 1778, I once more had the happiness of meeting my dear friends in London. The happiness I enjoyed was unspeakable.' The revivalism of America had never been congenial to him.

The year of the first Conference was the year when, as Carlyle says, Boston Harbour was ' black with unexpected tea.' Then followed the year of Lexington, and Concord, and Bunker Hill, introducing the War of Revolution with its years of conflict and suffering.

Francis Asbury and George Shadford consulted and prayed together. Should they stay or return to England ? Shadford decided that for him the call was clear that he should return. Asbury resolved to stay. ' If you are called to go,' he said, ' I am called to stay, so here we must part.' Even now one feels something like regret that Shadford did not stay. He had been one of the most successful of all the evangelists, as he was one of the most beloved. His sunniness and boyish love of fun, radiated happiness. He would have been just the kind of man that Asbury, with his fits of brooding and dejection, needed. The very presence of Shadford was a tonic. Native preachers sprang up under his inspiring ministry. Of all the men American Methodism could least afford to lose, excepting always Asbury, was George Shadford. But he went. It only remains now to reflect on what American Methodism would have been had Asbury gone too. He had however to go into hiding for a time. Judge White welcomed him to his home in Delaware, which was a refuge in the time of storm. Many of the Methodists suffered sharp persecution because of their connexion with the English missionaries.

The position had been made worse by the ill-advised pamphlet which John Wesley wrote. In an unhappy moment, his political bias and aristocratic haughtiness emerged. At first he admitted that the Americans had a grievance which justified their protests; but for some reason he changed his views and then unfortunately decided to publish them. He flung from his pen one of those incisive and crystal pamphlets which no one could write with a firmer hand than he. He called it *A Calm Address to the American People*. He seems to have been influenced by the papal and pompous effusion of Dr. Johnson, who had ventilated his intolerance in a book entitled *Taxation no Tyranny*. Many of Johnson's arguments were reproduced in Wesley's pamphlet. In such questions as these, Wesley should have known that Edmund Burke was a wiser guide than Samuel Johnson. Wesley adopted and adapted many of

Johnson's arguments. His unsympathetic point of view may be gathered from such a sentence as this ; ' There is most liberty of all, civil and religious, under a limited monarchy, there is usually less under an aristocracy, and least of all under a democracy.' He told the Americans that they were the descendants of men who either had no vote, or had resigned them by emigration. The mother country had a right to be reimbursed for some small part of the expense she had incurred. A small tax therefore was both legal and reasonable. The tone in which Wesley wrote was as unfortunate as his arguments. ' I will tell you,' he said, ' I speak the more freely because I am unbiassed. I have nothing to hope or fear on either side.'

Forty thousand copies of this untimely pamphlet were printed in three weeks. A large consignment found its way across the Atlantic, but a friend of Methodism, seeing well enough what havoc they would cause, got possession of them and destroyed them all. But America knew what the Founder of Methodism had written ; and to the impression created by such a publication must be set down the unpopularity both of Wesley, and often enough of the Methodists in America. Francis Asbury looked on, said little, and had grace and patience to bide his time. Happily by this time a race of native preachers had grown up, who by their vigour, their intelligence, and their devotion, matched the hour. Asbury remained in close concealment for only about five weeks ; and he travelled very little for eleven weeks ; but after that, for two years he was at large in Delaware before he recovered absolute freedom. The fact that he remained, helped to give him his pre-eminence in America. The rank and file honoured a fearless man, who had placed the interests of religion above those of patriotism, and who showed both by what he said and did that he perceived the inherent justice of the American claim.

We might pause here for a moment to look at Asbury's industry as a reader and a student, for it should never be forgotten that his virile ministry was sustained by a body of knowledge and learning which was the fruit of unremitting study. Dr. Schweitzer, who has as good a right as any living man to speak on this subject, tells us that 'the better a man's mental life and his intellectual interests are developed, the better he will be able to hold out in Africa.'[1] What is true of the missionary in Africa to-day, is true of all missionaries in all lands and all times. Asbury is a convincing illustration of this. He always had good books on hand. It was by steeping mind and heart in their calm wisdom, that he was himself lifted above the vexation and disappointments of his daily life. He read a hundred pages a day at least; it was this which helped to preserve the sense of proportion and the large vision, which made him an outstanding man wherever difficulties had to be discussed. Amid changing and fretful conditions, reading and prayer kept him steady. His *Journal* shows how widely he read; and from the bare record of travel, of work and of suffering we might select a passage or two, to illustrate his devotion to great thoughts and good influences. It will be sufficient to glean from the brief space of a few typical months, such references to reading as are to be found in his *Journal*. It should be remembered, too, that here we have nothing more than occasional notes. He was not called upon

[1] *On the Edge of the Primeval Forest*, p. 164.

THE REVOLUTION 93

to make a full record of all his mental industry. He read much of which we know nothing. On September 3, 1777, he says, 'My soul was watered with the peaceful influence of Divine Grace. . . . I spent much of my time in reading Law's *Serious Call*, and Baxter's *Call to the Unconverted*, and think the latter is one of the best pieces of human composition in the world to awaken the lethargic souls of poor sinners.' On Wednesday, November 12, we read : ' I now purposed, by the grace of God, as often as time will permit, to read six chapters every day in the Bible.' On January 11, 1778, there is the following entry : ' I have just finished the last volume of Josephus, and am surprised that at the age of seventy, Mr. Whiston should spend so much of his time in a dry chronological work. How much better was Mr. Baxter employed when he thought himself near to eternity, meditating and writing on the Saints' Everlasting Rest ! ' On the 23rd of the same month he says, ' I have found more sweetness and delight than ever in reading the Old Testament ; and having met with Luther's Comment on the Galatians, I have begun to read that.' On Thursday, March 5, he complains of a cold in his head and inflammation of his throat, which is an oft-recurring lament, but his time was ' chiefly spent in prayer, and Flavell's and Hartley's works, though no book is equal to the Bible.' On Monday, March 16, ' I applied myself to the Greek and Latin Testament.' On Thursday, April 9, he is busy with Alleine's *Letters*, and his soul was ' much comforted thereby.' The next day he writes, ' I have lately begun to read Mr. Wesley's *Notes* again, and have always found them, and his sermons, to be made an especial blessing to my soul.' On Wednesday, 22, he says, ' I finished my Wesley's *Notes*, and began to read Doddridge's *Rise and Progress.*' The next day he 'began reading honest John Bunyan's *Holy War.*'

This is enough to make it clear that Asbury was mentally eager, and still hungry for books. American Methodists to-day would probably all agree that the example set by Asbury as a student influenced and inspired the native preachers and evangelists, who gradually and affectionately raised him to the plane of a hero and an ideal.

Methodism in America was saved both from a superficial appeal to the emotions, and the heavy reaction which follows, through a devotion to learning. Asbury and his colleagues would not tolerate superficial and tawdry appeals, which aimed only at an immediate response on the part of the least instructed. There was a solid vein of informed common sense and erudition from the first. Had it not been so, the fires which began to burn so brightly, would have failed, and the revivals would have passed away like the morning cloud and the early dew. We have only to glance at the great centres of learning in America to-day, to see that the Church which rose up in the eighteenth century was a friend of truth and wisdom from the first. Men do not gather grapes of thorns, nor figs of thistles: and the Methodist Universities of to-day are as much the fruit of Asbury's steadfast love of good literature, and devotion to the study of languages, as the apple is the crown and fruit of the tree which bears it. Had there been on the part of those early preachers no serious study of the Bible, and no manly determination to master the outlines of Christian theology, the disintegrating elements of a disillusioned confidence would have resolved the

THE REVOLUTION

societies into scattered and struggling groups, presently to pass out of existence.

At the end of Asbury's references to his reading is a fitting place, however, to insert one of his burning sentences which show the saintly heart. 'Read fifty pages of Salmon's *Grammar*. It is plain to me *the devil will let us read always, if we will not pray.*' That is a sentence which searches the heart of every book lover.

The war dragged on. England showed the same capacity for making mistakes in war that she had shown in negotiation before war was declared. The end was inevitable. Cornwallis surrendered to Washington at Yorktown in October, 1781, and the United States came out of the conflict a new, a powerful, and a single nation.

The Conferences of 1774 and 1775 met in Philadelphia. The membership was stated at the latter to be 4,921; but when the Conference of 1778 was convened in Leesburg, Virginia, the desolations of war had declared themselves: there was a loss of 873 members and of eight ministers. There was, however, no loss of courage or of hope; six new circuits were adopted, and eleven probationers for the ministry received. The question of the administration of the sacraments was discussed once more, and once more was put aside for a future day. In the 'Minutes' of the next year (1779) there is the following significant paragraph:

> *Question* 12. Ought not Brother Asbury to act as General Assistant in America. *Answer:* He ought first, on account of his age, second because originally appointed by Mr. Wesley, third,

being joined by Messrs. Rankin and Shadford by express order from Mr. Wesley.

Question 13. How far shall his power extend ?
Answer: On hearing every preacher for and against what is in debate, the right of determination shall rest with him according to the Minutes.

Subjects likely to give anxiety were beginning to arise, and the South, particularly, was growing restive because there was no recognized provision for the administration of the Lord's Supper. Slavery also was a source of agitation : and it was far easier to say what was wrong, than to say how it could be put right. Asbury bore a heavy burden, but he had the inestimable gifts of patience and restraint. He was not willing that difficult questions should drift : but he knew that time often brings light, and he believed that with a firm dependence upon God, Methodism would see its way and do what was right.

It would be impossible in so brief a volume as this to give an account of the preachers who grew up in America, and were so eminently fitted to carry forward the great work ; but two or three names call tor special mention. The first native Methodist itinerant was William Watters. He was born in 1751 in Baltimore County. It was the preaching of Strawbridge and Owen that roused him as a lad of seventeen from complacency of soul to a deep concern about the new birth. When he was twenty he experienced a great spiritual change, and a year after began to preach. The Methodist leaders soon perceived his quality. They appointed him as an itinerant. He showed himself to be wise in winning souls. Arriving in Norfolk he soon formed a circuit which extended

THE REVOLUTION 97

for many miles around the town. His labours were abounding. Sickness did not vanquish him; and when he met Asbury he was inspired to pursue his high calling with even greater ardour.

The Methodist Church in America owes much to him. As much may be said also of Philip Gatch. Born the same year as Watters, they began their public labours together, and they were the two first American Methodist preachers reported in the 'Minutes.' Gatch has told the story of his conversion with the simple lucidity and confidence which characterized the testimony of nearly all the Methodists of that day. Rankin met him, and commissioned him as a preacher. We get glimpses of him as a mere youth of twenty-one, the first preacher sent as a regular itinerant to New Jersey. Perhaps with all his life of shining service, Gatch most readily commends himself to our hearts to-day for his noble testimony in relation to slavery. He came into possession of nine slaves, and he resolved at once to emancipate them, doing so in these imperishable words:

'Know all men by these presents, that I, Philip Gatch, of Powhaton County, Virginia, do believe that all men are by nature equally free, and from a clear conviction of the injustice of depriving my fellow creatures of their natural rights, do hereby emancipate and set free the following persons.'

Another of the early evangelists was Benjamin Abbott. The story of his conviction of sin, and all the struggles, and the fears he experienced before he found peace, is a moving one. His name, on a monument in Salem, New Jersey, testifies to the deep impression made by his ministry. He appears to have lived on the borderland which separates our prosaic life from the enchanted country where dreams, mysteries and visions are fashioned and leap into visibility. Southey, who rushed in with explanations, with no spiritual insight whatsoever, describes him as 'a strange half-madman.'

'Benjamin Abbott,' he says, 'not only threw his hearers into fits, but often fainted himself through the vehemence of his own prayers and preachments.' But Southey is no safe guide when men like Benjamin Abbott are to be discussed. It is true that Abbott was vehement, and sometimes crude in his preaching; but he was always intensely in earnest, and always preaching for the salvation of souls. Societies were formed through his labours. He worked for his livelihood on week-days but 'no itinerant in New Jersey did more to found securely the denomination in the State.' The testimony of Asbury was, ' He is a man of uncommon zeal, of good utterance: his words come with great power.' He has been called the ' John Bunyan ' of American Methodism.

Then there was Daniel Ruff, of Maryland. He was converted, and the year after his house, too, was converted into a ' preaching-place ' for the itinerants. He became an ' exhorter.' It was his sterling qualities of character, his simplicity, zeal and integrity that made him so successful. Asbury again may be quoted. 'Honest, simple, Daniel Ruff, has been made a great blessing to these people. Such is the wisdom and power of God that He has wrought marvellously by this plain man that no flesh may glory in His presence.'

If Daniel Ruff had no other claim to a place in the first half-dozen of the American Evangelists. it would be enough to recall that it was under his preaching,

THE REVOLUTION

Freeborn Garrettson was converted. To have won such a jewel for the Redeemer's crown made his life worth while. But he did more than that: he set an example of fidelity and love which gave him a warm place in the hearts of all his brethren.

These men, the first to take up the work of forming societies and circuits for Methodism in those early years, are but specimens of a long and shining list of heaven-sent apostles. We shall meet with some of them again, but for the most part their labours, their heroism, and the consecration which laid the foundations of the Methodist Church over whole colonies, must remain unrecorded. They wrought with single-minded devotion for the conversion of souls; and seldom has any ministry, in the whole history of the Christian Church been more immediately or richly rewarded.

CHAPTER VIII

THE SACRAMENTS AND ORDINATION

'The minister is much more than a leading brother as the Church itself is more than a fraternity. He is neither the mouthpiece of the Church, nor its chairman, nor its secretary. . . . He is not the servant, not the employee, of the Church. He is an apostle to it, the mouthpiece of Christ's gospel to it, the servant of the Word and not of the Church. . . . The ministry is a prophetic and sacramental office.'—FORSYTH—*The Church and Sacraments.*

WE have already alluded to the trouble that was brewing because the Sacraments were not administered in the Methodist Societies. It is true that Robert Strawbridge, with an Irishman's independence, and unfettered by any traditional devotion to the Anglican Church, had, with his immediate colleagues, taken the law into his own hands. He had founded societies in large numbers; and nearly one-half of the members of Methodism were in the regions where he and his loyal colleagues had exercised their faithful ministry. While Asbury and the Methodist preachers generally submitted to the deprivation, except when they could attend an Episcopal Church, Strawbridge firmly refused to depend on such precarious means of grace, or consent to the Methodist people having neither the Sacrament of Baptism for their Children, nor themselves enjoying the privilege of access to the Lord's Table. Why should he? The ministers of the Episcopal Church had most of them fled. Could it be

SACRAMENTS AND ORDINATION 101

that because there was no one who had been ordained or authorized by the Church of England to administer these Sacraments, that the only alternative was to be denied their blessedness altogether? Asbury's and Rankin's wishes were simply disregarded by Strawbridge; but somehow his decision lacked the reinforcement of general assent. The people did not rejoice in being admitted to the Lord's Table against the decision of the leaders of Methodism, nor would they consent to the spiritual privilege in any surreptitious manner. Hence the desire threatened to create serious trouble. We have seen that the first Conference, held in 1773, had laid it down very definitely that the brethren 'in connexion with Mr. Wesley' should avoid administration, both of the Sacrament of the Lord's Supper and of Baptism.

The situation was made the more acute now by reason both of the increasing numbers, and Asbury's loneliness as the sole representative of English Methodism. It testifies to the influence he exercised, and to the loyalty of his American colleagues, that, at a critical time, many of the latter refrained from following their own judgement and desire, in simple deference to his wishes. Asbury asked that they would wait; he hoped for light from Wesley. He felt sure a way out of the difficulty would be found. At one moment, however, it looked as if there would be general revolt on the part of the South, with a divided Methodism as the consequence. In 1779 two Conferences were held, one at the house of Judge White, Kent County, Delaware, on April 28, and the second at Fluvanna, Virginia, on May 18. The Northern Conference followed the lead of Asbury; but there was a good deal of apprehension as to what might be done in Virginia. The fear is expressed in the following quotation from the Minutes : ' Shall we guard against a separation from the Church direct or indirect ? *Answer :* By all means.'

The peril was not mitigated by the fact that the work was prospering with almost unprecedented success. There were revivals everywhere. To the confusion created by prosperity, was added that occasioned by the upheavals of the war—buildings had been destroyed, but societies had multiplied. It was seen by men like Asbury that at such a time nothing but ranks free from division, and moving in harmony and orderliness, could take full advantage of the running tide.

The Fluvanna Conference in Virginia, however, was resolute. They considered the burning subject and came to a decision which Asbury must have regarded as extremely menacing. They appointed a Committee consisting of the brethren Gatch, Foster, Cole and Ellis, and constituted these a Presbytery. This select group of leaders were to ordain one another in such manner as the Spirit of God seemed to direct, and then they were to ordain others who were eligible and ' were desirous of receiving ordination.' It was a fateful moment : and looking back, one trembles even now to see how nearly the work of God was wrecked by something more than a difference of opinion. Fundamental questions were involved. It seems almost a miracle that the Methodist Societies were not torn in twain at a time when there was no general and efficient organization to keep them in any kind of sympathetic relationship. A division at that time, and of such a nature, might easily have disrupted American Methodism, or have created two Churches

SACRAMENTS AND ORDINATION 103

so different in fundamental practice and policy as to have made future union almost impossible. Jesse Lee, who is the historian of this time, says of the Conference at Fluvanna that 'most of our preachers in the South fell in with this new plan; and as the leaders of the party were very zealous, and the greater part of them very pious men, the private members were influenced by them, and pretty generally fell in with their measures; however, some of the old Methodists would not commune with them, but steadily adhered to their old customs. There was great cause to fear a division, and both parties trembled for the ark of God, and shuddered at the thought of dividing the Church of Christ. But after all they consented, for the sake of peace and the union of the body of Methodists, to drop the ordinances for a season, till Mr. Wesley could be consulted.'[1] The resolve to wait awhile gave Asbury his opportunity. The northern preachers held a meeting in Baltimore in good time to appoint Asbury, Watters and Garrettson, as delegates to the next Virginian Conference. Asbury attended and read to them the letters of Wesley; he pleaded once more for a reasonable delay. The Conference seemed fixed in its determination to go forward. It looked as if Asbury had lost the day. He withdrew, as he says, 'with a broken heart,' and in a house near by poured out his soul in earnest prayer to God. Garrettson and Watters had also retired for prayer to another house. The end was all that Asbury desired: the brethren came to be of another mood and mind, and with an almost unanimous vote resolved to return to the old plan, give up the administration of the ordinances, and seek guidance or

[1] Stevens, *op. cit.*, p. 147.

methods which would accord with the wishes of
Wesley, and the desires of Asbury and those who felt
as he did. They further agreed all to meet in Baltimore
the next year. Meanwhile, Asbury, who had been
appointed General Assistant, was to seek the advice
of Wesley and spend the year in going through the
different Circuits, superintending and directing the
work and the workers. The numbers reported at
that time, as ' members of society,' were 10,539, with
twenty-five circuits, and fifty-five preachers.

The course of events now takes us back to England,
where we shall see how Wesley dealt with the crisis.
We shall find the great strategist once more ready for
the occasion, and prepared to follow the gleam where-
ever it led. One thing was clear to him and all his
colleagues ; it was that America must not be left to
struggle with a crisis, which would end in division
and possibly ruin. What then could be done ? Wesley
could not assent to the administration of the Sacraments by any man, unless he had been ordained
Vestiges of his high churchmanship clung to him to
the end. It is useless to criticize or debate the
question. With Wesley the limiting of the administration of the Sacraments to ordained men was
not an opinion, it was a principle, and too sacred to be
jeopardized. We may say, if we will, that Wesley's
way out of the difficulty was an extraordinary one.
It was : and he cannot be acquitted of a masterly
opportunism. The light fell upon his path, and he
walked with firmness and confidence. Asbury, holding
the views of Wesley, pleaded that ordained men
might be sent to supply the urgent need, and Wesley
was resolved not to turn a deaf ear to the request.
He had appealed to Lowth, the Bishop of London, to

SACRAMENTS AND ORDINATION 105

ordain a man named Hoskin, that he might go at once to America. There was throughout Wesley's life a vein of simplicity which is perhaps a feature of every great man's character. He might have known that bishops were not disposed to look with friendly eyes upon his irregular methods, or his multitudinous followers. So it was that the Bishop of London would not consent. He said that there were three ministers in America already and that he could not ordain the candidate sent up because he did not know enough Greek and Latin. This stung Wesley into a rejoinder which, to a fond Methodist, appears almost to enrich the literature of the world. Wesley was an old man now of eighty: he had retained such loyalty to the Church as the developments of Methodism would permit, and now, here was a Continent with multitudes of people truly converted, and asking for the means of grace, which the Sacraments alone supply. The Bishop treated the crisis with incredible levity. Wesley told him what he thought. What of the three ministers referred to by the Bishop already in America? 'They are men who have neither the power of religion nor the form: they have no claim to piety nor even decency.' And what about the Bishop's examination of candidates? 'Examining them!' says Wesley, indignantly, 'in what respects? Why whether they understand a little Latin or Greek, and can answer a few trite questions in the science of divinity. . . . My lord, I do by no means despise learning. I know the value of it too well. But what is this, particularly in a Christian minister, compared to piety. What is it in a man that has no religion? "As a jewel in a swine's snout." . . . Your lordship did see good to ordain and send to America other persons, who knew something of Greek and Latin : but knew no more of saving souls than of catching whales.' Whatever else such a letter might do, it ended all conversations with the Bishop, and closed the door to any further approach to the Anglican Church. But ' the resources of civilization ' were not exhausted. When Wesley could not travel along the path he desired, he found another way. He never sulked with providence : he believed in divine guidance all the time. It was this spiritual tractability which helped him out of his troubles.

This was in 1780 ; but more than thirty years before, as readers of his *Journal* know, Wesley had read a book while on the road to Bristol, which had been written by a young man who was afterwards to be Lord High Chancellor of England. Here are Wesley's words on January 20, 1746: ' On the road I read over *Lord King's account of the Primitive Church*. In spite of the vehement prejudice of my education, I was ready to believe that this was a fair and impartial draught, but if so, it would follow that bishops and presbyters are (essentially) of one order, and that originally every congregation was a church independent on all others.' The conviction was lodged there and then in Wesley's mind ; but not until Lowth had refused Wesley's appeal did the dormant seed begin to grow. What sun, rain and air are to the sleeping germ of life, such was the effect of the critical and exciting situation upon the slumbering truth that had been lying all these years in Wesley's mind. He said with the emphasis of firm conviction, ' If bishops and presbyters are one and the same in spiritual prerogative, I, who am a presbyter, may ordain, since bishops will not do so.' It was settled in his mind

SACRAMENTS AND ORDINATION 107

once and for all. The steps he would take were now clear. Wesley himself, with the help of one or two like-minded clergy, would lay their hands upon the heads of consecrated men, and send them forth to minister to the Methodists in America. Charles Wesley was distressed beyond measure at the proposal, but his brother was adamant when once he saw his way. It might safely be said that if Charles had had the direction of Methodism, it would have been crippled and paralysed from the first ; and that John knew quite well.

There was to be no delay. Who then were to be the candidates for such ordination ? This brings before us the interesting figure of Dr. Coke. ' A man of small stature, ruddy complexion, brilliant eyes, long hair, feminine but musical voice, and gowned as an English clergyman.' So he is described by the American historian. Coke, the son of a doctor, was born at Brecon, and had graduated at Oxford. He had considerable wealth, and freely used it to fulfil his holy mission in life. He first met Wesley while he was a curate at South Petherton in Somerset. After an interview with Wesley, which was evidently altogether delightful, he returned to his charge, and by the fervour and intensity of his evangelical preaching, did his best to turn the parish into a Methodist community. His fervour by no means pleased his bishop, his vicar, or his leading parishioners, and he was soon under notice to quit. His exit was celebrated by the ringing of the church bells, and with the crude generosity of his opponents, who provided hogsheads of cider that the people might enjoy themselves in an appropriate manner.

In the summer of 1777 Coke threw in his lot with

Wesley. He was then twenty-nine. He was to become one of Wesley's most distinguished and best-loved colleagues. The Methodist people took him to their heart at once. Coke soon showed that in every fibre of his being he was a missionary. He lifted up his eyes upon the world-wide harvest field ; and never rested until, on a May night in 1814, he suddenly died on board ship while on his way to Ceylon. Wesley read the heart of Coke, as he so quickly read the hearts of all spiritual pioneers. Clasping Coke's hands, he said : ' Brother ! go out : go out and preach the gospel to the whole world.' It was in the fulfilment of this grand behest that Coke was now about to engage. He was to play a conspicuous part in American Methodism in laying down those lines upon which the Church in that land was to be organized, and to develop.

On Tuesday, August 31, 1784, Wesley writes : ' Dr. Coke, Mr. Whatcoat and Mr. Vasey came down from London to embark for America.' An account of the remarkable events which preceded the departure of these three men is a vital part of our story. They had been ' set apart ' by Wesley, and a clergyman of the Church of England, the Rev. James Creighton, who was a member of Wesley's staff in London. It has often been pointed out, and sometimes set up as a subject for ridicule, that Wesley, who ordained Dr. Coke, might with equal fitness, have been ordained himself by his ordinand : for they were both presbyters of the Church of England. But Wesley was not a simpleton ; and while he may have been sometimes inconsistent, and sometimes imprudent, he was never absurd. The explanation of course is, that what Wesley did was, not to engage in a solemn act of

The Consecration of Francis Asbury as Bishop, 1784.

Richard Whatcoat and Thomas Vasey,
ordained by Wesley, September 2, 1784.

SACRAMENTS AND ORDINATION

ordination, which qualified Dr. Coke to administer the sacraments ; nor even to ordain him as a bishop ; but, with the laying on of his hands, and those of a brother clergyman, he set apart this radiant little man to be the *Superintendent* of the work in America. Coke may have had the desire to be a bishop : there is some reason to believe he had. Tyerman, who spares nobody, does not hesitate to attribute rather paltry motives to Coke, and says, 'he was dangerously ambitious.' But a bishopric was not in Wesley's thought at all, either for Coke or any other person.

He desired, however, that Coke should, in harmony with his own wish, be dedicated to a great and difficult work, and be able to take a leading part in straightening out the tangle which existed in America. It was in every way an advantage that Coke should go with the imprimatur of Wesley : and we may be sure all that Wesley intended was that Coke might, with the full weight and authority of Methodism behind him, assist in ordaining brethren in America, who would from thenceforth require no other qualifications.

Wesley did not use the term ' ordain ' in speaking of Coke, but ' set apart.' He did not hesitate to claim that in the case of Whatcoat and Vasey, their ordination was to be regarded as the equivalent of Episcopal ordination ; but his thought in relation to Coke is expressed in his own clear statement, which has the true Wesley ring in it, and is a challenge almost defiant in its uncompromising claim.

' To all to whom these presents shall come, John Wesley, late Fellow of Lincoln College in Oxford, Presbyter of the Church of England, sendeth greeting.

'Whereas many of the people of the Southern provinces of North America, who desire to continue under my care, and still adhere to the doctrine and discipline of the Church of England, are greatly distressed for want of ministers to administer the sacraments of baptism and the Lord's Supper, according to the usages of the same Church : and whereas there does not appear to be any other way of supplying them with ministers,

'Know all men that I, John Wesley, think myself to be providentially called at this time to set apart some persons for the work of the ministry in America. And, therefore, under the protection of Almighty God, and with a single eye to His glory, I have this day set apart as Superintendent, by the imposition of my hands, and prayer (being assisted by other ordained ministers), Thomas Coke, Doctor of Civil Law, a Presbyter of the Church of England, and a man whom I judge to be well qualified for that great work. And I do hereby recommend him to all whom it may concern, as a fit person to preside over the flock of Christ. In testimony whereof I have hereunto set my hand and seal, this second day of September, in the year of our Lord, one thousand seven hundred and eighty four.'

We can well believe that Coke felt himself doubly equipped as the bearer of such credentials.

Whatcoat and Vasey, who were ordained to be elders, were two of Wesley's preachers, and eight days before the three sailed, Wesley wrote a letter from Bristol, addressed 'to Dr. Coke, Mr. Asbury

SACRAMENTS AND ORDINATION

and our brethren in North America.' He states his views : and gives his reason for doing what he had done, and ends on this grand note : ' If any one will point out a more rational and scriptural way of feeding and guiding these poor sheep in the wilderness, I will gladly embrace it. At present, I cannot see any better method than that I have taken.'[1]

The ordinations, therefore, were the solemn act of one who was driven to the course he took, by the extremity and peril of the societies in America, and by the force of convictions, which, as we have seen, had been quietly cherished for thirty years. He held no theory of Apostolic Succession : he had seen too much of the working of God's Spirit among the people of England, through the medium of unordained men, to suppose that the fetters of what is vaguely called ' continuity ' were to be fastened upon the work of God. The same Lord who had intervened in the course of nature to fulfil His purposes, had again and again chosen simple men of dedicated hearts to carry out a work which had been neglected, and too often ignored, by those who were endowed by Episcopal ordination for its fulfilment. It is notorious that the clergy in America, before they returned to England as most of them did at the time of the Revolution, were spiritually dull or dead. ' I firmly believe,' said Wesley, '.I am a scriptural episcopos as much as any man in England, or in Europe : for the uninterrupted succession I know to be a fable, which no man ever did or ever can prove.' He would have agreed with Dean Inge, who calls it ' a fantastic and unhistorical theory.'[2] The firm decisions and the crystal-clear

[1] Tyerman, *op. cit.* III, p. 435.
[2] *Protestantism*, p. 57.

language of Wesley at this time show that he was still in the full possession of his marvellous powers of mind and will. There is no perceptible impairment of a single faculty. It will not do, therefore, for the critics who wish to explain away this awkward chapter in Wesley's life, to attribute his actions to the feebleness of age and natural senility.

It may be that Southey is right in saying, ' By arrogating the episcopal authority, he took the only step which was wanting to form the Methodists into a distinct body of Separatists from the Church.' That was a consequence which Wesley did not deliberately invoke: but one from which he would not shrink if he felt, as he did feel, that in the course he took he was following the guidance of the Spirit.

CHAPTER IX

THE METHODIST EPISCOPAL CHURCH

> *'My flesh sinks under labour. We are riding in a poor, 30-dollar chaise, in partnership, two bishops of us, but it must be confessed it tallies with the weight of our purses. What bishops! Well; but we hear great news, and we have great times, and each Western, Southern, and the Virginia Conference will have one thousand souls truly converted to God; and is not this an equivalent for a light purse? And are not we all paid for starving and toil? Yes: glory be to God.'*—ASBURY'S JOURNAL.

IN ordaining preachers Wesley had gone farther to cut himself off from the Church of England than by any previous act. We have seen what Southey had to say about these ordinations; but his verdict may be summarized in the words of the Rev. Henry Bett: 'Southey had neither enough spiritual discernment, nor enough breadth of general sympathy to write a fair account of a man whose conception of religion was so different from his own, and who was in every way (though Southey does not seem to have known it) so immeasurably greater a man than himself.'[1]

Wesley was as great a master with the pen, as in speech and action. He knew well enough that what he had done was unusual; and although he transcended the petty criticisms of his contemporaries by means of his own inherent greatness, and his simple faith in God, he was always ready to justify his

[1] Bett, *Studies in Literature*, p. 103.

actions ; and when good could be done thereby, he would set forth with the utmost perspicuity the grounds upon which he acted. It seemed wise to him that the three brethren who were commissioned for America should take with them a clear and full account of what had been done.

Accordingly he wrote a letter which, for every reason, is to be regarded as one of the historic documents of the Church. Iti s as follows :—

BRISTOL,
September 10, 1784.

To Dr. Coke, Mr. Asbury and our brethren in North America.

By a very uncommon train of providences many of the provinces of North America are totally disjoined from the mother country, and erected into independent States. The English Government has no authority over them, either civil or ecclesiastical, any more than over the States of Holland. A civil authority is exercised over them, partly by the Congress, partly by the provincial assemblies. But no one either exercises or claims any ecclesiastical authority at all. In this peculiar situation some thousands of the inhabitants of these States desire my advice, and, in compliance with their desire, I have drawn up a little sketch.

Lord King's account of the Primitive Church convinced me, many years ago, that bishops and presbyters are the same order, and consequently have the same right to ordain. For many years I have been importuned, from time to time, to

METHODIST EPISCOPAL CHURCH 115

exercise this right, by ordaining part of our travelling preachers. But I have still refused; not only for peace sake, but because I was determined as little as possible to violate the established order of the national church to which I belonged.

But the case is widely different between England and North America. Here there are bishops, who have a legal jurisdiction; in America there are none, neither any parish minister; so that for some hundreds of miles together there is none either to baptize, or to administer the Lord's Supper. Here, therefore, my scruples are at an end; and I conceive myself at full liberty, as I violate no order, and invade no man's right, by appointing and sending labourers into the harvest.

I have accordingly appointed Dr. Coke and Mr. Francis Asbury to be joint superintendents over our brethren in North America; as also Richard Whatcoat and Thomas Vasey, to act as elders among them, by baptizing and administering the Lord's Supper. And I have prepared a liturgy, little differing from that of the Church of England (I think the best constituted national church in the world), which I advise all the travelling preachers to use on the Lord's day in all congregations, reading the Litany only on Wednesdays and Fridays, and praying extempore on all other days. I also advise the elders to administer the Supper of the Lord on every Lord's day.

If any one will point out a more rational and Scriptural way of feeding and guiding these poor sheep in the wilderness, I will gladly embrace it. At present I cannot see any better method than that I have taken.

It has, indeed, been proposed to desire the English bishops to ordain part of our preachers for America. But to this I object : (1) I desired the Bishop of London to ordain one, but could not prevail. (2) If they consented, we know the slowness of their proceedings ; but the matter admits of no delay. (3) If they would ordain them now, they would expect to govern them ; and how grievously would this entangle us. (4) As our American brethren are now totally disentangled, both from the State and the English hierachy, we dare not entangle them again, either with the one or the other. They are now at full liberty, simply to follow the Scriptures and the primitive church. And we judge it best that they should stand fast in that liberty wherewith God has so strangely made them free.

With his mind thus expressed, and a heart serenely free from disturbing after-thoughts, Wesley went on his way, and Coke, Vasey and Whatcoat went on theirs. Coke appears to have been overflowing with happiness on the journey. The Life of Francis Xavier fed the fires of his soul. The ceaseless journeyings and unquenchable zeal of Xavier moved Coke to the depths of his being. ' O for a soul like his ! ' he cries out. ' But glory be to God, there is nothing impossible with Him. I seem to want the wings of an eagle, and the voice of a trumpet, that I may proclaim the gospel through the East and the West, the North and the South.'

METHODIST EPISCOPAL CHURCH 117

There is no record in detail of all that happened during the next few fateful weeks: but all that is essential to a full understanding of the founding of the Church has been preserved.

When Coke and his colleagues landed at New York on November 3, Asbury was as usual ' on the wing.'

Coke at once unfolded something of the plan which he would be prepared to submit, with the authority of Wesley, for the good government of the Church ; and John Dickens, an Eton scholar, and the Methodist preacher of the city, was delighted. Coke stopped in the midst of his exposition, realizing probably that it would be unseemly to tell the whole before he met Asbury. The meeting did not take place before Sunday, November 14. Coke and his friends had travelled as far South as Dover ; and on that day Coke, in company with Whatcoat, went to ' Barretts Chapel ' where he was to preach. The chapel was romantically situated ' in the midst of a forest ' and while Coke discoursed on the great text, ' But of Him are ye in Christ Jesus, who of God is made unto us wisdom, and righteousness, and sanctification, and redemption,' he was listened to by a large congregation. Among his hearers he says, was ' a plain robust man. After the sermon he came up to me in the pulpit and kissed me.' It was Francis Asbury. We can imagine the surging emotions in Asbury's heart. Here was a man from England : he was Wesley's colleague : he had come with good news : and he had shown the true Methodist instinct of making a bee-line for the great texts. The people generally, as we can well believe, were greatly affected by the spectacle of two such men greeting one another with such brotherly affection. ' Every heart appeared overflowing with love and fellowship,' says Ezekiel Cooper, ' and an ecstasy of joy and gladness ensued. I shall never forget the affecting scene.'

Asbury tells the story in his own dry and restrained fashion, and then adds a comment, which is not without its significance in this connexion. ' Having had no opportunity of conversing with them before public worship, I was greatly surprised to see Brother Whatcoat assist, by taking the cup in the administration of the Sacrament.'

But Asbury and Coke were soon in deep consultation. The plan was laid bare, and Asbury testifies to the amazement with which he heard some of Wesley's proposals ; one of which was that Coke, the presbyter, and Whatcoat and Vasey, the two ordained elders, should proceed to ordain him. ' I was shocked,' he says, ' when first informed of the intention of these brethren on coming to this country. It may be of God.'

But it was not long before Asbury yielded to the situation. He saw light at last. The threatened divisions would be avoided, the Sacraments would be administered, law and order would be secured, and a Church would be built up with all the elements of permanence and proportion.

The first thing to do was to summon the preachers from far and near. Freeborn Garrettson was to be the messenger. He sped off ' like an arrow,' summoning all his fellow preachers to gather at Baltimore for a General Conference. In six weeks he travelled twelve hundred miles, with his message, and when he returned he found that sixty preachers had responded.

The six weeks which intervened between the meeting

METHODIST EPISCOPAL CHURCH 119

in Barretts Chapel and the Conference, were not allowed to pass without a programme. Asbury made a plan for Dr. Coke, which involved a journey of a thousand miles. He provided Coke with a good horse, gave him a faithful negro servant, who was himself a true companion and an excellent preacher, and sent him on his way. This is exactly the way Coke would have chosen to spend his time. Travel was in his blood, and to be a pioneer for the gospel was the breath of life to him.

The General Conference began in the 'Lovely Lane' Chapel, Baltimore, on December 24, 1784. The occasion was momentous, but the building in which they met was but a crude structure. Dr. Coke, who presided, and who had known what comfort meant as well as endurance, expressed his thanks for the kindness of the people in providing a large stove to keep them warm, and backs to the seats on which they sat!

The first serious act of business, was to listen to the scheme, which had been largely drawn up in another land, and by the Founder of Methodism himself, for the organization of the Church. The brethren were excited by the prospect, and yet subdued by the solemnity of the thing they were about to do. Here was the vision of a Church before their very eyes, and in answer to their prayers. Until now they had been scattered societies, and unified only by a common concern, the salvation of souls. But they were not a Church. They had no sacraments, and no properly constituted and recognized authority. It was this for which they had been longing, and great was their joy as they saw the heaven-born creation come into visibility. Dr. Coke explained the proposals. There was nothing which could be called a debate. John Dickens, who was the most learned and scholarly man among them, as well as a powerful preacher, though Asbury used to say of him, 'he reasons too much,' moved the resolution that the plan should be adopted. It was agreed to by a unanimous vote ; the Methodist Episcopal Church of America was born.

The next act which captures the imagination is the ordination of Asbury.

He was not eager to be ordained as superintendent with Coke ; and although it was the express wish and instruction of Wesley, he would not consent until he had received the assurance of his brethren that it was their will. He was always afraid of honour, and power he prized only as an instrument with which to further the Kingdom of God. He knew that already he had an unsought influence and authority which smaller minds, in some instances, regarded with envy. But that which was the instruction of Wesley was also the fervent wish of his brethren. It was submitted to a vote, and Asbury was unanimously chosen to be the fellow superintendent with Coke. He was ordained deacon the second day of the Conference. Coke, Vasey and Whatcoat took part in the ordination. The next day, Sunday, Asbury was ordained an elder : and on Monday, Coke, with the assistance of his friend, Otterbein, a bishop of the German Church, consecrated Asbury as superintendent. The Conference proceeded for two or three days, to consider rules of discipline, and other matters which called for legislation. Several deacons were ordained, and on the following Sunday, January 2, twelve elders were ordained. Other matters were discussed : everybody seemed to be

METHODIST EPISCOPAL CHURCH 121

happy, and 'we ended,' says Whatcoat, 'in great peace and unanimity.' Dr. Ezra Tipple has given a list of many of the preachers present, with brief descriptions of their qualities, but the names have faded, and it is vain to recall men, whose chief distinction it was that they were Methodist preachers of proved loyalty and devotion. Reuben Ellis, Edward Dromgoole, John Haggerty, William Gill, Thomas Ware, Francis Portheyress, Joseph Everett: these are but names to us to-day. This cannot be said, however, of others. James O'Kelly, for example, has an unenviable immortality in that he became the fierce controversialist and the leader in a sharp and painful division. John Dickens is thus spoken of by Asbury in his *Journal*: 'For piety, probity and profitable preaching, holy living, Christian education of his children, secret prayer, I doubt whether his superior is to be found either in Europe or America.'

If any one of the members of that first General Conference ought to be singled out for special mention it should be Freeborn Garrettson. He was a native of Maryland, and his father was a man of influence and wealth. Strawbridge made a deep impression upon the mind of the lad, an impression which Asbury deepened. But it was under the ministry of Daniel Ruff that his spiritual awakening took place. He tells the story of his conversion. He was riding home one night, and his distress became a desperation of soul. He says, ' I threw the reins of my bridle on the horse's neck, and putting my hands together, cried out, " Lord, I submit." I was less than nothing in my own sight, and was now for the first time reconciled to the justice of God. The enmity of my heart was slain, the plan of salvation was open to me. I saw a beauty in the perfections of the Deity, and felt the power of faith and love that I had been a stranger to. My soul was exceeding happy that I seemed as if I wanted to take wing and fly away to heaven.'[1]

This is the authentic note. It was experiences such as this which made those early Methodists before all else evangelists. They had passed from darkness into light. Salvation had come to them after tears, struggles and despair. When they were set free, it was as though chains had fallen off. They were no longer under condemnation. Christ was their Saviour ; and so completely had He saved them that their love for Him sustained and inspired them in every kind of disappointment and hardship. Garrettson was received on trial in 1776, and for fifty years he never relaxed his toils. He travelled in the Carolinas, Pennsylvania, Maryland, Delaware, New Jersey and Nova Scotia. He had no other aim, and no other delight than preaching the gospel and winning souls to decision for Christ. He was frequently persecuted, and once was flung into Cambridge jail for a fortnight, where he says, ' I had a dirty floor for my bed, my saddle-bags for a pillow, and two large windows with an east wind blowing upon me, but I had great consolation in my Lord, and could say, " Thy will be done." ' Garrettson is one out of scores who were thus employed in the great work which was spreading so rapidly.

Before we pass away from the Conference of which men like these were members, we may glance at the duties and powers of the various orders of men ordained to their holy task.

The word superintendent soon gave place to the

[1] Stevens, *op. cit.*, p. 115.

METHODIST EPISCOPAL CHURCH 123

more scriptural word bishop, though truth compels us to suggest that Dr. Coke, probably, found a greater satisfaction in being addressed as bishop, than in the way Wesley had dictated. Apparently Wesley did not foresee that if a Church is to have deacons and presbyters, and to be known as the Methodist Episcopal Church, the term bishop would be almost inevitable. Superintendent had no ecclesiastical associations, and hardly suggested any dignity whatever.

Wesley, however, was angry when he heard of this new-born honour, and he wrote to Asbury, one of those merciless letters, which his friends were liable to receive when they grieved him. 'An instance of your greatness,' he says in addressing 'Dear Franky,' 'has given me great concern. How can you, how dare you suffer yourself to be called a Bishop. I shudder, I start at the very thought. Men call me a knave, or a fool, a rascal and a scoundrel, and I am content. But they shall never, by my consent, call me a bishop. For my sake, for God's sake, for Christ's sake, put a full end to this.'[1]

Asbury read the letter, and quietly put it aside. He knew whom to resist, and what to resent. It was not necessary to argue with Wesley. He was over eighty years of age, and more than two thousand miles away. They had tried in vain to get him to pay them a visit. The men on the spot had made their choice: and nothing in reason or Scripture opposed their decision. Bishops they were called, and bishops they have remained.

It is when we come to see the powers with which they were entrusted, and not the name by which they

[1] Lewis, *op. cit.*, p. 104.

were called, that we are surprised. The bishop presided over the Conference, and, says Dr. Stevens, 'he made absolutely the appointments, or annual distribution of the preachers, having yet no " Cabinet " of presiding elders, a species of Council, which usage has since established, though it has no recognition in the Discipline. In the intervals of Conference he could receive, charge or suspend preachers. He decided, finally, appeals from both preachers and people. Ordinations depended upon the majority of the Conference, but the Bishop had a veto power over any such vote.'

The other two orders were at first designated ' Assistants and helpers '; but this nomenclature went the way of ' Superintendents.' They soon became known as ' elders ' and ' deacons.' The elder was ' to see that the other preachers in his circuit behave well and want nothing, to renew the tickets quarterly and regulate the bands; to take in or put out of the Society or the bands,' and generally to act as the bishop's assistant. The ' helpers ' were not permitted on their first appointment to administer the Lord's Supper.

As soon as the Conference had broken up Asbury was on the long trail again. The proceedings ended on Monday, January 3, 1785: on Tuesday he rode ' fifty miles through frost and snow.' On Thursday he says, ' We had an exceedingly cold ride to Prince William—little less than forty miles.' It is worth while to note that the first sermon Asbury preached after his ordination, was from the text, ' Unto me, who am the least of all saints, was this grace given, to preach among the Gentiles, the unsearchable riches of Christ ' (Eph. iii. 8).

Asbury at Drew Seminary.

Dr. Coke's visit lasted for five months. He and Asbury were true yoke-fellows, though there is reason to suppose that the relationship was not always perfectly harmonious and undisturbed. Coke was no doubt ambitious, restless, and at times incalculable. Nor need we suppose that Asbury, with his brooding temperament, his frequent dejection, his ulcerated throat and his intractable organs, was always radiant as an angel.

Happily no difference between these two bishops was ever more than a temporary ruffle of the otherwise placid waters. Moreover, Coke was always more or less a bird of passage : he came and went ; he crossed the Atlantic eighteen times ; but Asbury had his home in America ; and he wanted no other in this world.

The Church was now a fact. When we think of the country, its spirit of independence, the wide reaches over which the Methodists operated, and the raw condition of multitudes who were brought within its membership, we are bound to acknowledge that the men who were its leaders must have possessed natural qualities of a superior kind. It would have been easy to blunder or to admit disintegrating influences which would steadily sap the Church's constancy and power. The Church was saved by the sanity of its leaders, and the revivals, which were almost a regular feature in every part of the vast field over which its mission extended. The triumphs of redeeming grace witnessed continuously, kept the hearts of their preachers warm, and constituted the one concern of every society. This lesson, writ large on the pages of American Methodism, is one which our own Church to-day should take to heart.

CHAPTER X

THE GENERAL CONFERENCE

'*A fear rose in my mind of what might be the event of this. But it was soon banished by considering " I must go on and mind my own business, which is enough for me ; and leave these things to the providence of God."* '
ASBURY'S JOURNAL.

THE Methodist Episcopal Church now reposed on foundations which had been well and truly laid. The members of the General Conference had returned to their Circuits. Methodism was spreading with unprecedented rapidity. It numbered now some eighteen thousand members, with a hundred and four itinerant preachers, to say nothing of the hundreds of local preachers and exhorters, whose services can never be too highly valued. ' It is safe,' writes Dr. Stevens, of this moment, ' to estimate the Methodist community at about two hundred thousand, including all habitual attendants on its worship.' More than sixty chapels had been built. A mere recital of the Colonies which had been invaded, is illuminating. New York, West Jersey, Pennsylvania, Maryland, Delaware, Virginia, Georgia, The Carolinas, Tennessee and Kentucky, were all attacked. When the Conference was over, Asbury and Coke travelled together for the few months of Coke's visit ; and Asbury, after providing Coke with a first-class horse, does not seem to have spared his companion. They went practically from one end of the States to the other. Asbury, who

THE GENERAL CONFERENCE 127

writes of hair-breadth escapes, as though they were normal features of the day's march, says they 'had to swim upon their horses several times.' The roads were hardly worth the name, the forests were well-nigh impenetrable: there were bogs and swamps through which they had to struggle, and poor Dr. Coke came to have the profoundest admiration for the preachers who had habitually to overcome these difficulties and terrors. He says, ' The preachers ride here about a hundred miles a week, but the swamps and morasses they have to pass through it is tremendous to relate. Though it is now the month of April, I was above my knees in water on horseback in passing through a deep morass, and that when it was almost dark. . . . In travelling, our rides are so long that we are frequently on horseback till midnight.'[1]

The two bishops, as the result of their cogitations and companionship, resolved upon a daring act: they would call on General Washington, offer their felicitations, and invoke his aid in dealing with slavery. The war had ended, and Washington had, to his own great delight, returned once more to his home, Mount Vernon, in Virginia. Asbury and Coke must have known how sore England still was : and they probably foresaw that this simple act of homage would create some displeasure in the homeland ; but Asbury was safe, when two or three thousand miles away, and Dr. Coke was not the kind of man to sacrifice an immediate pleasure which came in the guise of duty, because of a possible criticism which might or might not arise, but which in any case he would not have to face for some months.

It is a pleasing picture, that of these two Methodist

[1] Stevens, *op. cit.*, p. 186.

dignitaries visiting the wisest and noblest man in America, who cared little for honour and less for power, and yet would presently be called upon, now that he had won the war, to take the foremost place in the councils of peace.

Mr. H. G. Wells speaks of Washington as 'a conspicuously indolent man.' The verdict is unnecessarily severe, but Washington himself is largely responsible for its adoption. He ostentatiously placed his love of home in the forefront of his programme. It is hardly to be wondered at ; for any one who visits Mount Vernon to-day and wanders about the house and grounds, which are preserved in their primitive and exquisite simplicity, can understand Washington being happy in such a spot, and requesting that, in the end, there his bones should be laid to rest. There he and Martha Washington made home a delight, and Nature had done her best to make it a paradise with trees, gardens, and sun-kissed slopes gently declining to the beautiful River Potomac. The stately language of Washington, when he was torn once more from Mount Vernon, deserves to be recalled :

I was summoned by my country, whose voice I can never hear but with veneration and love, from a retreat which I had chosen with the fondest predelection and in my flattering hopes, with an immutable decision as the asylum of my declining years.'[1]

Asbury and Coke called on Washington as representatives and leaders of the Methodist Church. ' He received us,' says Coke, ' very politely, and was very open to access. He is quite the plain country gentleman. After dinner we desired a private inter-

[1] *New York Daily Gazette*, May 1, 1789.

THE GENERAL CONFERENCE 129

view and opened to him the grand business on which we came, presenting to him our petition for the emancipation of negroes and entreating his signature, if the eminence of his station did not render it inexpedient for him to sign any petition.'[1] But Washington was not to be entangled by a hurried signature. He saw well enough that slavery was so woven into the very texture of the nation as to require patience, courage and the general co-operation of the whole community. Washington begged his visitors to stay the night, which they were unable to do. But while he made it clear that he loved slavery as little as they did, he did not judge it the wise thing to attach his signature to this particular petition. It was to the credit of Asbury and Coke to call and so worthily represent the aspirations of Methodism, but either they did not foresee the place that Washington was yet to occupy in the States of America, or else they acted upon the maxim of asking the utmost and being content with whatever was granted.

Coke sailed for England a day or two later, and no doubt had to explain to his exacerbated countrymen, who could acknowledge neither the superior forces of Washington, nor the logic of events. He and Asbury, it was said, had betrayed the dignity of Britain. It was a storm in a teacup: at any rate Asbury was undismayed. It is certain that Coke also was not deeply distressed at the criticisms he had had to face, for when four years later (1789) he was again in America he repeated the indiscretion.

By this time Washington had been made, without intention or desire on his part, the first President of the United States, and Asbury and Coke once more

[1] Stevens, *op. cit.*, p. 184.

paid him a visit. This time, however, they were to be the bearers of a message which had the full weight and authority of the Conference which met in New York 1789. Asbury suggested a congratulatory address: the Conference approved, and two selected brethren went off to make arrangements with the President for the formal presentation of the greeting. The address, which was read by Asbury, and the reply of Washington were as follows :—

To the President of the United States.

SIR,

We, the bishops of the Methodist Episcopal Church, humbly beg leave, in the name of our Society collectively in these United States, to express to you the warm feeling of our hearts, and our sincere congratulations on your appointment to the Presidentship of these States. We are conscious, from the signal proofs you have already given, that you are a friend of mankind, and, under this established idea, place as full confidence in your wisdom and integrity for the preservation of those civil and religious liberties which have been transmitted to us by the providence of God and the glorious Revolution, as we believe ought to be reposed in man.

We have received the most grateful satisfaction from the humble and entire dependence on the great Governor of the universe which you have repeatedly expressed, acknowledging Him the source of every blessing and particularly of the most excellent Constitution of these States, which is at present the admiration of the world, and may in future become its great exemplar for imitation ;

THE GENERAL CONFERENCE 131

and hence we enjoy a holy expectation, that you will always prove a faithful and impartial patron of genuine, vital religion, the grand end of our creation and present probationary existence. And we promise you our fervent prayers to the throne of grace, that God Almighty may endue you with all the graces and gifts of His Holy Spirit, that He may enable you to fill up your important station to His glory, the good of the Church, the happiness and prosperity of the United States, and the welfare of mankind.

> *Signed*, on behalf of the Methodist Episcopal Church,
>
> THOMAS COKE,
> FRANCIS ASBURY.

New York, May 29, 1789.

'The Glorious Revolution' showed what American Methodists felt, and they did not hesitate to praise the Constitution, which may or may not have been 'the admiration of the world.' Washington's reply shows that such sentiments were welcome.

> *To the Bishops of the Methodist Episcopal Church in the United States of America.*

GENTLEMEN,

I return to you individually, and through you to your Society collectively in the United States, my thanks for the demonstration of affection, and the expression of joy offered, in their behalf, on my late appointment. It shall be my endeavour to manifest the purity of my inclinations for promoting the happiness of mankind, as well as the sincerity of my desires to contribute whatever may be in my power toward the civil and religious liberties of the American people. In pursuing this line of conduct, I hope, by the assistance of divine Providence, not altogether to disappoint the confidence which you have been pleased to repose in me.

It always affords me satisfaction when I find a concurrence of sentiment and practice between all conscientious men, in acknowledgement of homage to the great Governor of the universe, and in professions of support to a just civil government. After mentioning that, I trust the people of every denomination, who demean themselves as good citizens, will have occasion to be convinced that I shall always strive to prove a faithful and impartial patron of genuine, vital religion. I must assure you in particular that I take in the kindest part the promise you make of presenting your prayers at the throne of grace for me, and that I likewise implore the divine benediction on yourselves and your religious community.

GEORGE WASHINGTON.

The exchange was natural and manly, but it was not allowed to pass without sharp resentment in America, as well as at home. It is thought that certain critics on the American side were stung into annoyance because the Methodists had forestalled them. The hectic protests, however, were short-lived : and no one now would say that the Conference did not do the right and seemly thing.

When the first General Conference met in 1784 it

THE GENERAL CONFERENCE 133

was for a specific purpose as we have seen, and at its close no one appears to have foreseen that it would be followed after eight years by a second, and thenceforth by a similar gathering every four years. As a matter of fact, Asbury wanted a Council; and the New York Conference of 1789 grudgingly approved. The Council was to be composed of men selected by himself, who should have almost plenary powers.

The first of these Councils was held the same year. Eleven preachers were present besides Asbury. A good deal of useful work was done, but it is to be feared that the trouble which was already brewing was aggravated by this most unpopular institution. It met only once more : this time in December, 1790. Few of Asbury's proposals were so ill-advised ; even he had to learn all over again the lesson which a man of growing influence and power so readily forgets, that where a large number of men share hardships and work, they expect to share also the responsibility and delights of power.

A General Conference therefore met in 1792. The necessity for it was obvious. The Annual Conferences were able to deal with questions which had local significance, but it was important that subjects of universal interest should be dealt with by a body of people representing the whole extent of the area. The rapid development of Methodism at this period is almost incredible, and only a firm, wise rule could give to the multiplying societies the coherence and stability which were essential.

Coke returned from a visit to England in 1792. He had left the year before on hearing of Wesley's death, but after the brief period indicated, returned in time to preside over the Conference. A great deal had

134 DAWN OF AMERICAN METHODISM

happened in the eight years which separated the first General Conference from the second. For one thing it had been made clear that the Americans were still men of an independent spirit. John Wesley appears to have regarded the Conference and preachers generally as subject to his control. He had given instructions that Whatcoat should be made a superintendent, but the Conferences would not take orders. They discovered in Whatcoat, surprisingly enough, a lack of experience, and affected to believe the appointment an unsuitable one. The Conference in 1784 had given Wesley some reason to suppose that his word would be unquestioningly obeyed. Asbury sat silent, but with some misgiving of heart, as that Conference declared themselves Wesley's 'sons in the gospel' and ready to 'obey his commands.' It should not have required Asbury's shrewdness to have seen that such an affirmation might well suggest to Wesley an authority which would be either resented or prove unreal. When, therefore, Wesley gave instructions for a Conference to be held in Baltimore on May 1, 1787, that Whatcoat should be raised to the dignity of a superintendent, and that Freeborn Garrettson should be appointed to have charge of the work in Nova Scotia, the annoyance developed into a revolt, and in a fit of indignation they passed a resolution to drop Wesley's name from their minutes. What Wesley thought of this may be judged from such a sentence as the following : ' It was not well judged of Brother Asbury to suffer, much less directly encourage, the foolish step of the last Conference.'

The storm was over in two years, and at the end of that time the Conferences were wise enough to restore Wesley's name. The entry on their Minutes runs :

William McKendree.
Bishop 1808.

Freeborn Garrettson.

THE GENERAL CONFERENCE 135

Question 1. Who are the persons that exercise the episcopal office in the Methodist Church in Europe and America ? *Answer :* John Wesley, Thomas Coke and Francis Asbury, by regular order and succession.

There is something almost droll in these relenting brethren, not only restoring Wesley's name to their ' Minutes ' but in bestowing on him the rank of a bishop, and giving him a diocese which embraced Europe.

Wesley was always a little disposed to treat his colleagues as children not quite grown up ; and as he grew older the weakness was more pronounced. It seemed to him the right and natural thing that such a young body as the American Methodists would be more in need of his paternal supervision than were his sons in the gospel in England. But the republicans had not fought for their freedom as citizens without taking something of the same spirit into their Church life. When Dr. Coke, for example, as a bishop, presumed to alter the date of a Conference to suit his convenience, while still in England, he was made to understand in no uncertain manner that such dictation would not be tolerated and he ' gave a solemn written engagement to keep himself from administering affairs when absent from the United States, to ordain and to preside at Conferences when in the States, and to keep himself to those things only, and to travelling at large. This was given on May 2, 1787.'[1]

It is one of the curiosities and ironies of history that Wesley, who should have denounced the use of the term bishop, desired the superintendent to be

[1] Lewis, *op. cit.*, p. 111.

clad as nearly as possible like one, and that the Americans, while adopting the name he rejected, refused the gowns and bands he offered. In the emphasis of their refusal they abjured all clerical dress whatsoever. We happen to know, from a contemporary record, the kind of dress Asbury and Whatcoat wore. ' The bishops Asbury and Whatcoat were plain, simple, venerable persons, both in dress and manners. Their costume was that of former times, the colour drab, the waistcoat with large laps, and both coat and waistcoat without any collar ; their plain stocks and low-crowned, broad-brimmed hats bespoke their deadness to the trifling ornaments of dress. In a word, their appearance was simplicity itself.'[1]

Visitors to an American Conference to-day would find the same simplicity, with, perhaps, a touch of fashion which the first bishops disdained. The present dignitaries may be said to resemble prosperous members of the Stock Exchange in dress, rather than the elaborately adorned bishops of our own country.

The abbreviated Prayer Book which Wesley had proposed was treated much in the same way. What the clergy of the Church of England may have thought of Wesley's treatment of the Book of Common Prayer can only be surmised ; but he did not hesitate to lay somewhat violent hands upon its sacred pages for the edification of American Methodists. He omitted most of the Holy Days, shortened the form of service for the Lord's Day, altered the offices for Baptism and the Burial of the Dead, and omitted fifteen of the Articles of Religion, and several Psalms. There is a modern note in his observation that many of these

[1] *New History of Methodism*, Vol. II, p. 110.

THE GENERAL CONFERENCE 137

were 'highly improper for the mouths of a Christian congregation.' That was his present to America. The proper comment on this is to quote from an eye witness, who was present at a Conference at Union Town, July, 1787. It was an ordination service and has an added interest in that it is said to have been the first Methodist ordination beyond the Alleghanies. James Quinn writes : ' Mr. Asbury officiated, not in the costume of the lawn-robed prelate, but as the plain presbyter in gown and band, assisted by Richard Whatcoat, elder in the same clerical habit. The person ordained was Michael Leard, of whom it was said that he could repeat nearly the whole of the New Testament from memory, and also large portions of the Old. The scenes of that day looked well in the eyes of the Church people, for not only did the preachers appear in sacerdotal robes, but the morning service was read as abridged by Mr. Wesley. The priestly robes and Prayer Book were, however, soon laid aside at the same time, for I have never seen the one, nor heard the other since.'[1]

When on Friday, April 29, 1791, the news of Wesley's death reached Asbury, he allows his mind to run back over the years, and his *Journal* vibrates with the emotion of one who owed more than words could say to the departed leader. ' I conclude his equal is not to be found among all the sons of Adam he may have left behind, Brother Coke was sunk in spirit, and wished to hasten home immediately. For myself, notwithstanding my long absence from Mr. Wesley, and a few unpleasant expressions in some of the letters that the dear old man has written to me (occasioned by the misrepresentations of others) I feel the stroke

[1] Stevens, *op. cit.*, p. 188.

most sensibly, and I expect I shall never read his works without reflecting on the loss which the Church of God has sustained by his death.'

The course of events has taken us now to Baltimore, when the second General Conference was held in 1792. Dr. Coke had returned, and he presided over the Conference. It was to be observed that the relations between him and Asbury were less cordial than formerly. The reason appeared in the Conference itself, when James O'Kelly lodged his protest against the methods which Asbury and others employed. This hard and bitter controversialist had written to Wesley with the unscrupulousness of a fierce partisan, and undoubtedly thereby disturbed Wesley's peace of mind; Wesley, in turn, it is thought, had conveyed his doubts and fears to Dr. Coke. It is believed, indeed, that it was at Wesley's firm request that Coke should assist in putting an end to the Council which had created so many heart burnings among those most easily disaffected.

The main question which was to be debated at the second General Conference must be reserved for another chapter; and the present one may be concluded with another brief review of the ever-increasing numbers gathered into the Methodist Church. The returns at the Christmas Conference of 1785 showed 14,988 members, and eighty-three preachers. Five years later these figures had to be altered to 57,631 members, and 227 preachers. When we advance another two years, that is to the moment of the Conference in 1792, we find 65,980 members and 266 preachers. The average annual gain over a period of eight years was not less than 6,374 members and that of the preachers, even at a time when men retired

THE GENERAL CONFERENCE 139

without being superannuated, twenty-three. It is pleasant to recall, that Barbara Heck, Captain Webb, Joseph Pilmoor and George Shadford, all lived to rejoice in these triumphs of grace. There are surely few stories in the whole glowing history of the Christian Church which recount such constant advances, accompanied both by a development in organization, and the evolution of a ministry of such mighty moral and intellectual power as this.

These great souls never rested, were never satisfied : they built wisely and they kept on building. At no moment did they grow slack by feebly talking about ' consolidation.'. Each man was a herald : and grand old Asbury, for he seemed an old man early, led both in precept and example.

In 1786 he spoke of himself as, ' Poor, coughing, wheezing Francis Asbury.' He was then just forty-one, and another thirty years of unremitting toil lay before him. He was known as the man who rambled through the United States. ' I come,' he said, ' from Boston, New York, Philadelphia, Baltimore or almost any place you please.' If ever a man was a bishop, Asbury was one.

CHAPTER XI

TROUBLES AND TRIUMPHS

' I cannot praise a fugitive and cloistered virtue, unexercised and unbreathed, that never sallies out and sees her adversary, but slinks out of the race, where that immortal garland is to be run for, not without dust and heat.'—MILTON—*Areopagitica*.

WE may be permitted to remind the reader that when an attempt is made in so brief a volume as this, to set forth the opulent story of early American Methodism, attention is necessarily centred upon strategic movements and critical events, but all the while we are conscious of a background of supreme importance. It is easy to describe a Conference, and the movements therein which affected the structure and form of the Church : but it is far from easy to do justice to the faithful work of godly men and women, without which all such Conferences are in vain.

The thought which is continually with us as we follow the more spectacular incidents is that, year in, year out, in all kinds of weather, and with almost every concomitant of hardship, there was a race of men, whose names may be, for the most part, forgotten, but who never ceased to pursue the great tasks of evangelism. If we pause for a moment, putting aside the problems and tasks of statesmanship and its expression, we can almost hear the songs of converted people in rude chapels, in forest huts, and in the open air, rejoicing together in the knowledge of sins for-

TROUBLES AND TRIUMPHS 141

given. American Methodism produced men of rugged power and great ability, whose chief joy it was to promote revivals wherever they went. The large additions to the Church must not be primarily ascribed to the decisions of a Council or the Conference: they were rather the fruits of ceaseless toil on the part of brave and consecrated men, who had only one theme and only one aim. The material which Conferences had to handle was provided by the preachers, the class leaders, the exhorters, and all that host of radiant people in whose faces the light of heaven shone. We may not be able to give biographies of Valentine Cook and Jesse Lee, of Peter Cartwright and Lorenzo Dow, of Abner Neal and Enoch George, but to such heralds of the cross, we must ascribe the astonishing chapters which are the distinction and the glory of this great spiritual movement.

It might have been foretold, from what one knows both of human nature and of history, that such a rapidly-multiplying community, with all the vigour and daring of a spiritual rebirth, would require firm guidance and continual correction. The very abundance of life is itself a peril; and so it was that when the preachers gathered for the second General Conference at Baltimore in 1792, there were both the rumblings of disaffection, and the quickening impulses of far-reaching proposals.

Eight years before, at the first General Conference, John Dickens had brought forward a scheme for the establishment of a School. The idea was cordially accepted and approved. Asbury from the first gave his support, and Coke was enthusiastic. We shall see that this first venture in educational enterprise was not a success; but the eagerness for education itself, which was its driving power, was not extinguished by a single failure. Asbury never lost his fierce regard for education ; he saw that, if the Church was to enlist all the powers of man, opportunity must be provided to impart the elements of learning, and to fortify the zeal of the ministry by a knowledge which would withstand criticism, and probe to the depths of truth.

It would be difficult indeed to do justice to the zeal for education, which was to be a conspicuous feature of the Methodist Church. It was a tradition with the American people. The Puritans were the patrons of education. The pioneers who had come from England and had laid the foundations of the eastern colonies, were men who cared supremely for schools and every educational advantage for their children. The Methodists set to work at once. Six months after the first Annual Conference, on June 5, 1785, the foundations were laid of ' Cokesbury College,' at Abingdon, Maryland. The site was a singularly beautiful one. Just twenty-five miles from Baltimore, it commanded enchanting views which stretched in some directions for more than forty miles. The Susquehanna Valley lay open before it, while away in the distance could be seen the gleaming waters of Chesapeake Bay.

John Wesley heard of the project, and scented a touch of human vanity in the name. ' Cokesbury ' was an amalgam, which enshrined the names of the two bishops and ' College ' suggested ambitions which he thought to be too high-flying. Events proved him to be right. Again Wesley flew to his pen, and again he told ' Dear Franky,' with paternal plainness, what he thought of this. ' I study to be little, you study

TROUBLES AND TRIUMPHS 143

to be great. I creep, you strut along. I found a School, you found a College. Nay: and called after your own names!' This was probably one of 'the unpleasant letters' which Asbury pensively recalled when he heard of Wesley's death. The grandiose features of the College were of Coke's invention. Years later, when Asbury had to contemplate the ruins of the enterprise, he said, 'I wished only for Schools. Dr. Coke wanted a College.'

From the first the College was a burden. Asbury more than once went from house to house, in cold and snow, begging for its support. His *Journal* is fretted at many points with the troubles that the College gave him. On Monday, October 22, 1792, he writes, ' Rode to Cokesbury; all is not well here.' For some mysterious reason the finances were never sound and no one in charge seems to have had any appreciation of the unyielding rigour of pounds, shillings and pence. It is not the first, and by no means the last, instance of men well versed in education, and highly qualified to teach advanced subjects, who are babes in finance. Asbury discovered on one of his visits that over £700 had been spent in five months. The College was not without a degree of popularity, and there is no reason to say that it did not minister in many ways to the well-being of the Church. The children of the ministers were educated there, and the itinerants often availed themselves of its hospitality; but it lasted only ten years. It was built too soon, and on a scale too costly. It never enjoyed a wholesome and life-giving freedom from debt. Before even it was opened, a liability of £900 rested upon it. Asbury was troubled, too, as much about the spiritual indifference of those in charge as about the money. 'If we cannot have a Christian School,' he says, 'that is a School under Christian discipline and pious teachers, we will have none.' The end of it all came after ten years of struggling life. 'Cokesbury College,' Asbury wrote in his *Journal*, 'is consumed to ashes, a sacrifice of £10,000 in about ten years . . . Would any man give me £10,000 per year to do and suffer again, what I have done for that house, I would not do it . . . I feel distressed at the loss of the library.'

The shadow of this abortive enterprise lay upon the second General Conference, but the matters which engaged the chief attention of the assembly were of another kind.

James O'Kelly was ordained in 1784, and from the first showed himself to have the shrivelled sympathy and persistent bitterness of a troubler in Israel. As so often happens with such a man, he was not without reasonable grounds for his attack, and was, for that reason, supported by men of larger vision and finer abilities than his own. It was the first sharp controversy in any of the Methodist Conferences, and it acquired point and fierceness from the fact that censure was directed against its greatest man. It will not be a surprise to learn that the power given or claimed by the bishops was the root of the trouble. Dr. Coke presided over the Conference, and Francis Asbury hardly spoke at all, largely through indisposition, but partly too, we may suppose, from policy. He knew how to be silent, and had an intense dislike of what he called 'the disease of disputation.' The fact that the resolution which O'Kelly submitted was supported by men of such commanding authority as

TROUBLES AND TRIUMPHS 145

Freeborn Garrettson, Richard Ivey and Hope Hull, proves it to have had much in its favour. It read thus: 'After the bishop appoints the preachers at the Conference to their several circuits, if any one think himself injured by the appointment, he shall have liberty to appeal to the Conference and state his objections: and if the Conference approve his objections, the bishop shall appoint him to another circuit.'

There is something fair and equitable in the substance of such a resolution; but obviously, if it were carried under such a leader, aiming as it did both at the conduct and the authority of Asbury, it would have been a blow from which even he might not have recovered. The battle of debate lasted for several days. Coke appears to have been so entranced with the eloquence and general debating power of the assembly, as at times almost to have forgotten the issues involved. In the end the resolution was defeated by a large majority. It was probably Asbury's stainless record and acknowledged probity, which saved the resolution; and it has been the consistent conformity of the American bishops throughout with this lofty example, which has preserved their power without diminution. 'I am happy,' was Asbury's comment, 'that I never stationed a preacher through enmity, or as a punishment. I have acted for the glory of God, the good of the people, and to promote the usefulness of the preachers.' With all that, an English Methodist will still wonder if such a system could be introduced into this country, or if so, whether it could be maintained for more than a year. It may not be without interest to quote in this connexion some words written by Dr. Howard after the General Conference in Atlantic City, as recently as 1932. ' In recent years,' he says, ' a rising tide of opposition to the Episcopate has been felt, and many declare that the office, valuable as it was in the pioneer days of American Methodism, is out of tune with modern democratic principles. But as many of the most greatly beloved ministers are elected to the Episcopate, and as it is but rarely that the protest, " Nolo episcopari " is heard, the Church seems likely to be governed in this way for many years to come.'[1] With such an inconclusive statement, we can allow the powers of the bishop, and the future of the Episcopate, to be dealt with by those who may be called upon to handle them.

O'Kelly lost his cause, and sat down at once to write his resignation. Others, unfortunately, joined him in this rather human form of resentment and reprisal. He gathered his friends about him, and formed what was called ' The Republican Methodist Church.' The split was fruitful in misery to all concerned. Asbury reflecting on the causes of the deplorable division, says : ' One wanted to be immovably fixed in a district ; another wanted money ; a third wanted ordination ; a fourth wanted to do as he liked about slaves.' It was more than the wisest man could do to satisfy so many discontents. It seems a pity now that some form of Church Government was not adopted, which distributed both the responsibility and the power among a group of men, rather than to lay it upon the shoulders of poor, over-worked, and ailing Francis Asbury.

O'Kelly's followers soon failed him ; as, no doubt, in vision and in moral loftiness, he soon failed them.

[1] *Methodist Recorder.* May 26, 1932.

TROUBLES AND TRIUMPHS 147

American Methodists may well rejoice that one of the younger men, McKendree, who at first joined O'Kelly, soon returned to the bosom of the mother Church. He was to be Asbury's colleague and son, and to prove himself one of the greatest of a number of very able men.

We need not pursue the story of the Methodist Republican Church. Its history was a series of lamentable experiments and failures. From the first moment it began to disintegrate. O'Kelly had done his worst, and he added greatly to the hardships which Asbury so patiently bore. There is a touching glimpse of Asbury's forgiving spirit to be seen in an incident of 1802. O'Kelly was ill, and Asbury sent to know if a visit would be welcome. The answer assured him. He went, and in the bedroom the two sat and conversed. There were the general inquiries after one another's health, they talked of persons and things indifferently. Then, without a word of former troubles, they prayed, and Asbury went on his way again. No mention was made of former troubles. One of the historians, under the influence, we suppose, of an active imagination, speaks of O'Kelly as then upon his deathbed; but Dr. Stevens tells us that he lived long after this; and, unfortunately, illness did not cure his perverseness of temperament. He was, more or less, a storm-centre to the day of his death, which did not take place until he had long passed his ninetieth year.

The passing years told their tale upon the strength of Asbury. The Churches grew and multiplied, while his own powers of endurance naturally diminished. The kind of life he had so bravely lived, naturally impaired his strength, and though he lived to be more than seventy, he was often laid aside, and still more often working when a less strenuous minister of the gospel would have been at home in the hands of the doctor.

At the Baltimore Conference of 1800 the question of another bishop had to be faced. Coke was often in England ; and even when in America he was not always a kindred spirit with Asbury. What, therefore, could one man do, with a diocese of such magnitude ? The Church was without precedents, and the questions, therefore, which had to be determined were whether the Conference should elect another bishop, to share equally with Asbury, the authority and the burdens of the episcopate ; and if so, upon whom the choice should fall. After some random and fantastic suggestions, it was agreed that another bishop should be chosen. The choice then lay between two men, Richard Whatcoat and Jesse Lee. If natural ability alone had to be considered, no doubt Lee would have been elected. His name has a lustre which shines to this day. No one seems to have been more untiring or more devoted than Lee. He was an eloquent preacher, a fearless pioneer and a wise counsellor. But Whatcoat's claims were of a transcendent order. It was his character which won the hearts of all. Without guile and without ambition, he pursued his work, with a constant rejoicing in the Lord. All his contemporaries seem to require the word ' saintly ' to describe him. When the decision was taken at the Conference Whatcoat received four votes more than Lee. When presently he was consecrated, the comment of Henry Boehm was, ' Never were holy hands laid upon a holier head.' Dr. Coke preached the ordination sermon. This may be regarded as the last service Coke was to render the American Methodists upon

TROUBLES AND TRIUMPHS 149

their own soil. Whatcoat was a choice soul. To the best of his failing powers he helped Asbury; but it was apparent that this man, who had already been in the ministry for nearly forty years, had not the strength to do all that was needed. He pursued his work with a placid and tireless persistence. He is said once to have baptized seventy-five children in a single day. Wherever he went he ingeminated peace and good will. When he passed away in 1806, Asbury, whose eulogies are always restrained and conscientious, said of him: ' That father in Israel; my friend for forty years; a man of solid parts, a self-denying man of God, whoever heard him speak an idle word ? '

It may be as well at this point to round off in a few paragraphs our references to Asbury himself. The glimpses we have given of this distinguished servant of God have served, we hope, to indicate the grandeur of his character, and the superior quality of his service. Through all those trying and tumultuous years he was the firm figure around which less constant spirits rallied. In tireless labour, in patient attention to details, in quenchless evangelism and in holy living, he was the inspiration and exemplar to all his brethren in the ministry. He never married. He was as sensitive to comfort and as appreciative of little acts of kindness as any man. Few comforts came his way. The joys of home appealed to him : but he never had one. He tells us why. He noted early in life that men who married happily, were a little too fond of the amenities of the fireside for the exacting work of a Methodist minister. ' I calculate,' he said, ' we have lost the travelling labours of two hundred of the best men in America, or the world, by marriage and consequent location.'

Towards the end of his life he wrote what may be called an apologia, with reference to his celibacy. It is a firm and strangely moving document, which must be quoted at length :

'If I should die in celibacy, which I think quite probable, I give the following reasons for what can scarcely be called my choice. I was called in my fourth year ; I began public exercises between sixteen and seventeen ; at twenty-one I travelled ; at twenty-six I came to America ; thus far I had reasons enough for a single life. It had been my intention of returning to Europe at thirty years of age ; but the war continued, and it was ten years before we had a settled, lasting peace ; this was no time to marry or be given in marriage. At forty-nine I was ordained superintendent bishop in America. Amongst the duties imposed upon me by my office was that of travelling extensively, and I could hardly expect to find a woman with grace enough to enable her to live but one week out of the fifty-two with her husband ; besides, what right has any man to take advantage of the affections of a woman, make her his wife, and by a voluntary absence subvert the whole order and economy of the marriage state, by separating those whom neither God, nature, nor the requirements of civil society permit long to be put asunder ? It is neither just nor generous. I may add to this that I had little money, and with this little administered to the necessities of a beloved mother until I was fifty-seven ; if I have done wrong, I hope God and the sex will forgive me ; it is my duty now to bestow the pittance

TROUBLES AND TRIUMPHS 151

I may have to spare upon the widows and fatherless girls, and poor married men.'

His last years were cheered in many ways, though he continued to bear hardness as a good soldier of Jesus Christ. Whatcoat's company was a solace and an inspiration. Later McKendree was a son to him. ' Brother McKendree,' he says, ' made me a tent of his own and John Watson's blankets, and happily saved me from taking cold, whilst I slept two hours under my grand marquee.'

He prized, too, the affection of children : and there were many of these who loved to welcome him ; they had come to regard him as children do a grandfather, and his benignant and tender ways won all their hearts. But what kept him in good heart, more than all else, was the continual and rapid growth of Methodism. From 1800 to 1804 the membership was doubled. Nothing sufficed to turn him away from his one great concern, the salvation of souls. He resolved to ' preach sanctification in every sermon,' but he was always pleading for decisions. He saw that nothing less than a new birth in Christ was sufficient.

As the years pass, there is the same submissive resignation on the approach of old age, with its enfeeblement, which we find in the *Journal* of John Wesley. ' I have pains in my body, particularly in my hip, which are very afflictive when I ride ; but I cheer myself as well as I may with songs in the night —with Wesley's, Watts' and Stennett's Sight of Canaan in four hymns.'

' My eyes fail. I will resign the stations to Bishop McKendree—I will draw away my feet. It is the fifty-fifth year of ministry, and forty-fifth of labour in America. My mind enjoys great peace and consolation.'

Henry Boehm, his friend, has left a description of his personal appearance for which we have good reason to thank him. ' Five feet nine inches high : erect in person and of a very commanding appearance. His features were rugged, but his countenance was intelligent, though time and care had furrowed it deep with wrinkles. His nose was prominent, his mouth large, as if made on purpose to talk, and his eyes of a bluish cast, and so keen that it seemed as if he could look right through a person. He had a fine forehead, indicative of no ordinary brain, and beautiful white locks which hung about his brow and shoulders and added to his venerable appearance. There was as much native dignity about him as any man I ever knew. He seemed born to sway others. There was an austerity about his looks that was forbidding to those who were not acquainted with him. In dress he was a pattern of neatness and plainness.'

This was the man whose ministry and influence are recognized throughout two continents to-day. When he died on March 31, 1816, he was in his seventy-first year. The funeral was at Baltimore. Twenty to twenty-five thousand people gathered to pay their tribute. Perhaps the eulogy of President Coolidge, will outlive all other words spoken in honour of this great servant of Christ. When, on October 16, 1924, a great assembly met at Washington for the unveiling of the beautiful equestrian statue to Asbury, Coolidge said, ' Who shall say when his influence, written on the immortal souls of men, shall end ? How many homes must he have hallowed ! What a multitude

TROUBLES AND TRIUMPHS

of frontier mothers must have brought their children to him for blessing !

'It is more than probable that Nancy Hanks, the mother of Lincoln, had heard him in her youth. Adams and Jefferson must have known him, and Jackson must have seen in him a flaming spirit as unconquerable as his own.

'How many temples dot our landscape? How many institutions of learning, some of them rejoicing in the name of Wesleyan, all trace the inspiration of their existence to the sacrifice and service of this one circuit rider. He is entitled to rank as one of the builders of our nation.'

CHAPTER XII

EVANGELISM AND EDUCATION

'*Long my imprisoned spirit lay
  Fast bound in sin and nature's night;
Thine eye diffused a quickening ray,
  I woke, the dungeon flamed with light;
My chains fell off, my heart was free,
I rose, went forth, and followed Thee.*'
                                    CHARLES WESLEY.

WE have now reached a stage in the development of American Methodism where it becomes impossible to follow its progress in detail. The itinerants continued to extend the frontiers of their kingdom, with each new-created State. It is true there was a serious decline in numbers for a few years, consequent upon the O'Kelly secession. It is computed that the loss from 1792 to 1796 was not less than nine thousand; but presently the traces of that division faded out, and the story of a triumphal progress was resumed.

We have only to turn to the voluminous pages of Dr. Stevens' history to see how greatly favoured was the Church in the preachers she had grown. Even so patient and elaborate a historian as he, found it difficult to do any kind of justice to the men whose lives of devotion and manifold gifts, entitle them to a secure place in the affections and gratitude of the Church.

One man, however, we must pause to glance at —William McKendree. For every reason he has a foremost place in the story of those years. He was endowed with such a variety of exceptional qualities,

EVANGELISM AND EDUCATION 155

as to constitute him the natural leader of his Church in succession to Asbury. We have seen that when O'Kelly led away a few of the preachers, McKendree was one of them. He was not satisfied, however, with the step he had taken. There was something in O'Kelly which his keen eye detected, and could not approve. Moreover, he recalled what he had seen of Asbury, and felt he ought to take steps to know the bishop better. Accordingly he withdrew his resignation, and at the same time resolved to find out for himself Asbury's true spirit, and the nature of his methods. With this in mind he accompanied Asbury on his travels, and soon discovered the greatness and the goodness of the bishop. McKendree had, like so many of the preachers, passed through an experience of soul which can only be described as a sudden transition from darkness into light. 'I ventured my all upon Christ,' he said. 'In a moment my soul was relieved of a burden too heavy to be borne, and joy instantly succeeded sorrow.' The memory of such a miracle was an abiding inspiration, and it gave point and unction to his preaching. He believed what had happened in his life was possible in the lives of others. Hence his preaching had the confident and urgent note of a sinner saved by grace, whose one desire it was to see others saved, too. The Methodist preachers were all evangelists : there is no other secret of their success. As soon then as McKendree had recovered his belief in Asbury's wisdom and high purpose, he came also to love him with the affection of a son : and it is comforting, as we pursue the pilgrimage of the enfeebled and suffering bishop, to know that he was protected and watched over by the loving solicitude of this young man.

McKendree was a strong man in every way. He had a powerful frame, 'Nearly six feet in height, of extraordinary strength and activity, fair complexion, black hair and blue eyes. His intellect as a whole was bright and his thoughts diamond-pointed.'[1] That is the description of a contemporary admirer, who rejoiced in the virility and conspicuous gifts of McKendree. Asbury soon gave him as much work as he could do. He judged McKendree to be the man to take charge of the precious and thriving societies of the Mississippi Valley, whither the immigrants were pressing, and increasing, with amazing rapidity. There McKendree took up the work. 'He never said foolish things—never weak, never even common things. There was thought in all his words, and wisdom in all his thoughts. He was the man for the times and the age in which he lived, leading in triumph the Church in the wilderness.'[2] He laboured in other districts, notably in Virginia; always with the same cheerful devotion; always with the same inspiring effect on others, and always with the same success. He was the kind of man other men both admire and love. As an example, when Jesse Lee was dying, among his last words were, 'Give my respects to Bishop McKendree, and tell him that I die in love with all the preachers, that I do love him, and that he lies in my heart.' He was the first of all the American preachers to be appointed a bishop. It is often said that McKendree made his election sure by a single sermon. Probably this means nothing more than that one who had in a hundred ways already shown his superlative gifts, now convinced the hesitating, or the uninformed, so

[1] Stevens, *op. cit.*, p. 259.
[2] *Ibid.*, p. 259.

Luckman's Statue of Francis Asbury in Washington, D.C.
By the kindness of Mr. H. H. Prince.

EVANGELISM AND EDUCATION 157

that a general agreement was precipitated, and McKendree was elected.

The description by Dr. Nathan Bangs of McKendree and his sermon, on the memorable occasion when he took all hearts by storm, is so vivid that it cannot be passed over. It was at the General Conference of 1808 in Baltimore. The Church was crowded.

> 'The second gallery at one end of the chapel was crowded with coloured people. I saw the preacher of the morning enter the pulpit, sunburnt, and dressed in very ordinary clothes, with a red flannel shirt, which showed a large space between his vest and small clothes. He appeared more like a backwoodsman than a minister of the gospel. I felt mortified that such a looking man should have been appointed to preach on such an imposing occasion. In his prayers he seemed to lack words, and even stammered. I became uneasy for the honour of the Conference and the Church. He gave out his text: " For the hurt of the daughter of My people am I hurt; I am black; astonishment hath taken hold of me. Is there no balm in Gilead ? Is there no physician there ? Why then is not the health of the daughter of my people recovered ? " As he advanced in his discourse, a mysterious magnetism seemed to emanate from him to all parts of the house. He was absorbed in the interest of his subject, his voice rose gradually until it sounded like a trumpet; at a climactic passage the effect was overwhelming. It thrilled through the assembly like an electric shock; the house rang with irrepressible responses; many hearers

fell prostrate to the floor. An athletic man, sitting by my side, fell as if hit by a cannon ball. I felt my own heart melting, and feared that I should also fall from my seat. Such an astonishing effect, so sudden and overpowering, I seldom or never saw.' [1]

It is easy to imagine the suffused glow, and the happy ejaculations of the preachers, when they became aware of such a man in their ranks.

> Then felt I like some watcher of the skies,
> When a new planet swims into his ken.

He is one of the men not so well known on this side of the Atlantic as he should be. Built on ample lines, he was endowed with a powerful personality, an acute intellect, and the level judgement of a statesman. Like Asbury he never married. In McKendree's day the Church, of course, was no longer a small group of undistinguished or unknown men, as it was during the major part of Asbury's ministry. He was the first among equals: and there were many preachers of clear intellect, and superb qualities of mind and soul.

The reference to the strange physical consequences of McKendree's preaching leads naturally to some consideration of what was a feature of the meetings in those days, and especially to the camp meetings as they were called. It was quite a common thing for people listening to the gospel to lose consciousness, or to be transported with ecstacy, and apparently be unable to control either their limbs or their speech. Thomas Rankin had looked on these outbursts with cold disdain: Asbury never encouraged any

[1] *New History of Methodism*, Vol. II. p. 118.

EVANGELISM AND EDUCATION 159

eccentricity or saw, necessarily, in strange physical contortions the evidence of the Spirit's working : but he had the quiet, tentative, and inquiring spirit of John Wesley himself, when things happened which he did not understand. McKendree, however, had grown up among the people, and was better able to appreciate the emotional impact of powerful preaching. He was undisturbed when people fell under his preaching like soldiers on the battlefield, or shouted and danced with no evident control of themselves. He knew when God was working in the midst of the people ; he could overlook extravagances : his one desire was that there should be a genuine work of grace in the hearts of the people. Let him be sure of that, and he did not trouble.

We have to remember, too, that the congregations were not the disciplined, inert and gospel-hardened people of modern England. They were backwoodsmen, and pioneers, in many instances. The mellowing effect of civilization and city life had not chastened them into a bland self-control. There was also the effect upon mind and heart of the vindictive Indians to be taken into account, when we analyse the reactions of the people. Many of these Indians lived on the edge of a settlement, the character of whom David Garnett has shown us, in his delicate romance, *Pocahontas*. Murders were common and too frequently the murderer could not be traced. The scalped bodies of victims were a common sight in the pathways of the wilder parts. In spite of perils, the people kept pressing further and further westward, and Methodism followed them. The preachers so engaged were men who knew the habits of the people, and could appreciate their hopes and fears. Happily in America, as in this country, Methodism knew how to use the unusual man. One such man was Peter Cartwright, and a brief reference to his autobiography, may be excused because of the authentic glimpses it affords of the conditions, in which men like him exercised their powerful ministry.

Peter Cartwright himself was a child of the woods. He was fashioned by nature for pioneer work among the backwoodsmen. In his romantic story he reveals a personality of rugged power, who aimed fearlessly at a great objective, and sometimes adopted the most unconventional methods to reach it. The picture he gives us of himself, as well as of the scenes and conditions in which he laboured, is true to life. Perhaps no other book extant, tells us so graphically what we want to know. The whole panorama is before our eyes: the wild and unsubdued country, the stealthy Indians, the benighted backwoodsmen, and the scrambling immigrants. Only a resolute man of iron constitution could carry on such work as he did year after year. He and his fellow workers had not simply to meet the darkened minds of the people generally: but there were all kinds of false teaching to be countered. Such a country, in such a state as was the heart of America at this time, supplies a breeding ground for every variety of spiritual quack and impostor.

It is worth our while to transcribe a characteristic passage from J. B. Finley, a contemporary of Cartwright, and himself a frontiersman with a full share of daring. We have to envisage a camp meeting with thousands of people listening. Peter is one of many preachers, but few had such natural eloquence, and imagination as he.

EVANGELISM AND EDUCATION

'He began with a loud and beautifully modulated tone, in a voice that rolled on the serene night air like successive peals of grand thunder. Methodist ministers are celebrated for their voices, but his was matchless in sweetness as well as power. For the first ten minutes his remarks, being preparatory, were commonplace and uninteresting, but then, all of a sudden, his face reddened, his eyes brightened, his gestures grew animated as the waftures of a fierce torch.'

For a time, Peter seems to have been playful and humorous ; and then when his vast congregation had composed themselves in the genial atmosphere, the preacher once more suddenly changed, and, says Finley, ' His features lost their comical tinge of pleasantry ; his voice grew first earnest and then solemn, and soon wailed out in the tones of deepest pathos ; his eyes were shorn of their mild light, and yielded streams of tears as the fountain of the hill yielded water. The effect was indescribable . . . He then made a call for mourners into the altar, and five hundred, many of them till that night infidels, rushed forward and prostrated themselves on their knees.'[1]

The camp meeting itself was a feature of those days. Vast numbers gathered together. Notices were sent out several weeks in advance, and at the set time the crowds began to gather. Some of them had come hundreds of miles. Asbury himself was always at home in a camp meeting. He tells us that at times as many as ten thousand people would be present, and not less than three hundred travelling preachers. A thousand conversions were sometimes recorded in a single week. If a fastidious critic of to-day should

[1] *The Autobiography of James B. Finley*, p. 322.

feel disposed to dissect such an institution and expose its dangers, the answer is—the American Methodist Church of the present day. The meetings would last sometimes for three or four weeks. Sometimes as many as twenty or thirty preachers would be holding forth at the same moment. Some had a wagon for their pulpit, others found a platform in the fork of a tree ; while for others a natural eminence was sufficient. It was no picnic. The multitude gathered hungering for the bread of life. There would, of course, be a scoundrel here and there ; Peter Cartwright made short shrift of all such when they came into his vicinity. He would knock down a man and then pray with him. When at last the camp meeting broke up, the people, hundreds of them with a new song in their hearts, returned to their clearings, and their homes, to reinforce the little struggling Methodist Society already in existence, or to form a new society, destined to be the nucleus of a powerful Church. Many of the thriving and resourceful Churches which are now so numerous in the Mississippi valley and elsewhere, can trace their ancestry to the converts who found the Saviour at a camp meeting.

As we have seen, a frequent feature of such meetings was the overwhelming effect of the preaching upon the hearers. Finley tells us of himself : ' My heart beat tremendously, my lips quivered and I felt as though I must fall to the ground.' He went into the woods to recover possession of himself and on returning saw ' five hundred people swept down in a moment, as if a battery of a thousand guns had been opened upon them.' Peter Cartwright says, ' I have seen more than a hundred sinners fall like dead men under one powerful sermon, and I have seen and heard more

EVANGELISM AND EDUCATION 163

than five hundred Christians all shouting aloud the high praises of God at once.'[1]

These psychical effects may still await an adequate explanation, but as readers of Wesley's *Journal* know, they are not peculiar to early Methodism in America. Both the person who explains away the phenomena, and the one who denounces them, may be disregarded. Similarly any one who discredits the reality of the spiritual transformations which so often accompanied them, shows that he has no intimate knowledge of either American or English Methodism.

We can only do justice to the leadership and the vision of those early Methodist leaders by bringing into our picture their ceaseless regard for the instruction of the young, which showed itself in the provision made for their education. Men like Peter Cartwright might taunt Colleges with producing anaemic or ineffective men; but the leaders, with comprehensive views and a sense of proportion, did not share such narrow views. Of Asbury, who was not a College bred man, we might say, as was finely said of an early Methodist leader of this country, ' His strong love of learning amounted almost to genius; he had the manners of one nobly born and the aptitudes and instincts of a scholar.'[2] Cokesbury College may be written down as a failure: but the reasons for this have been given. It was incautiously devised by one whose genius was not so sure and far-seeing as Asbury's; moreover it was premature. But let any one travel through the States to-day and he will see, not only Churches of majestic proportions, but Methodist Colleges and Universities, the roots of

[1] *Autobiography*, p. 14.
[2] *James Thorne*, by F. W. Bourne, p. 99.

which are to be found in those far-off days of struggle. While these great institutions keep pace with modern learning, they owe their birth in many instances to the insight and unselfishness of men, who knew that their own usefulness and power would have been greatly increased, had they been equipped from the first with the knowledge and learning, for which they continued through life so ardently to strive.

It might be said that the love of learning in early American Methodism amounted almost to a passion. In less than fifty years from the founding of the Church, ' Book Concerns ' as they are called, were established ; and magazines of sterling quality had achieved large circulations.

The list of Institutions, all designed to promote education, almost surpasses belief. In 1830, both the Wesleyan University at Middletown, Connecticut, and the Randolph Mason College in Virginia were founded. The Emory and Henry College in Virginia dates from 1836, as does also the Wesleyan College in Georgia. It is proudly claimed for the latter of these, that it was the first College founded for women. Emory College in Georgia also dates from 1836. The evolution of this College, which has produced the Emory University of to-day, is a process which any Englishman, who walks amid her palaces at Atlanta, might fervently pray to be repeated in our own land. The marble buildings testify to great generosity, and a true appreciation of the part education must have in fitting men to develop and fashion the fine instrument of the human mind for the highest purposes in the Kingdom of God.

We have not given a complete list by any means, for happily it is no part of our task to describe the

EVANGELISM AND EDUCATION

Methodism of the United States in its powerful operations to-day. What we have said should suffice to indicate that the evangelism which appealed to benighted souls, making the spiritual wilderness to rejoice and blossom as the rose, was under the direction of men who recognized that the love of God, if it is not to be as the morning cloud and early dew, must be sustained by the mind as well as the heart. Nor is it any refutation of this, to call attention to the backwaters of Fundamentalism, which still lodge in some parts of the States. The Methodist Church has welcomed the light : even when some of her timid, though devout souls have feared for the Ark of God. We have no desire to justify obscurantism, but in fairness to all, it should be conceded that attacks have sometimes been made in the name of learning, which do not appear to have either a seemly regard for men entitled to respect, or any adequate appreciation of the grave issues involved. Methodism in America has been jealous for a sound and godly education, and still is.

CHAPTER XIII

THE SUNDERED CHURCH

' *With malice toward none ; with charity for all ; with firmness in the right, as God gives us to see the right, let us strive on to finish the work we are in ; to bind up the nation's wounds ; to care for him who shall have borne the battle, and for his widow, and his orphan—to do all which may achieve and cherish a just and a lasting peace among ourselves, and with all nations.'*—ABRAHAM LINCOLN—*The Second Inaugural Address.*

FROM the earliest days of Methodism in America the ministers and members of the Church were troubled by the existence of slavery. Allusions to it run like a sad refrain through the whole of Asbury's *Journal*: ' I know not which to pity most,' he said, ' the slaves or their masters.' The Methodists had hardly begun to meet in Conference before they began also to pass resolutions on the subject. These were not always well considered perhaps, but they were always well intentioned. In 1780, for example, the Conference required the preachers holding slaves to set them free. It declared that ' this Conference acknowledges that slavery is contrary to the dictates of conscience and pure religion, and doing that which we would not that others should do to us and ours.'

Five years later there was a call for ' the extirpation ' of slavery. It was more easy to call for it than to command it. Slavery was woven into the whole texture of the commerce and life of the States. But no one could rest : every one felt there was something

THE SUNDERED CHURCH 167

sadly wrong; though just what to do, passed the wit of any Conference.

A most historic, but perhaps hasty, resolution was passed at the General Conference of 1800, laying it down that 'if any of our travelling preachers marry persons holding slaves, and thereby become slave holders, they shall be excluded from our Societies, unless they execute a legal emancipation of their slaves agreeably to the laws of the State wherein they live.' The resolution was passed by men of fine ideals, who did not fully appreciate what were its implications. In the same spirit, in 1812, the General Conference in New York resolved that 'no slave holder shall be eligible to the office of local elder in any State or Territory, where the civil laws will admit emancipation, and suffer the liberated slave to enjoy his freedom.'

In their attitude to slavery the Methodists were by no means alone. Other Churches shared their concern: and, indeed, it is the Quakers who must be regarded as pioneers in the cause of emancipation. Under the leadership of such men as John Woolman and Anthony Benezet, they 'stood clear of slave-holding before the end of the eighteenth century.'[1] At their London yearly meeting of 1761 they decided that 'all members concerned in the traffic should be disowned.'[2]

The struggle began early: but it was not until a civil war had drenched the nation in blood that the slaves were set free throughout the nation. To the acutest and most sensitive minds of America, the presence of the slave was a menace and a humiliation. Washington kept slaves, but he deplored slavery:

[1] Brayshaw, *The Quakers*, p. 79.   [2] *Ibid.*, p. 179.

and if this is accepted as proof of his inconsistency, it is also an illustration of the perplexity in which many other citizens of undoubted probity found themselves. They did not like to see any man a slave : but they did not know how to do without the work which the slave did, nor did they know what to do with the slave himself. Wesley, writing from our side of the Atlantic, in the last of all his clean-cut letters, said to Wilberforce, ' Go on : in the name of God and in the power of His might, till even American slavery, the vilest that ever saw the sun, shall vanish away before it.'[1] It was far easier to write like that in England, than to see a way to the emancipation of the slave in America. Slavery was reinforced by arguments of undoubted cogency. The people who lived among the negroes saw how primitive and childish were their thoughts, and how elementary their mental development. They saw, too, how ill-equipped they were even for liberty, to say nothing of giving them an equal place with their owners. Many believed it as a truth, not to be disputed, that the negro race was designed by providence to be the slave of the white man. The equality of the human race might be acknowledged as a truth embedded in the Gospel, but in such a world as this, with all its rude inequalities, perils and needs, all that could be expected as a working creed, was the obligation to care for the slave with consideration, and shelter him both from the cruelty of the oppressor, and the consequences of his own ignorance. The New Testament did not appear to them to be conclusive. Christ did not denounce explicitly the slavery of His day ; and Paul did not definitely require of Philemon that

[1] Tyerman, *op. cit.*, III. p. 114.

THE SUNDERED CHURCH 169

he should set Onesimus free. Whatever reflections on slavery seem proper to us at this time of day, as Englishmen, we have little right to reproach America. We upheld the system for many centuries, and by means of it built up not a little of our commercial prosperity. Lord Dartmouth wrote in 1776 that the ' Colonists should not be allowed to check or discourage a traffic so beneficent to the nation.'[4]

Liverpool, Bristol and London ports were busy with the slave traffic. No less than 192 ships plied to and fro in the interests of the slave owner. These ships were declared to provide accommodation for 47,146 slaves. The misery involved in a transport so inadequate in humane accommodation, can hardly be imagined. The poor creatures had not even room to lie down, and when rough weather drove them into shelter, there was hardly space to breathe. But did it matter seriously? If they died it was a loss to their owners certainly, but the sea was a convenient grave. If they lived, they would ultimately reach a land where they would have the amenities of work without wages, and shelter without home! Fresh from the glades and forests of Africa, where they had been tracked down by cunning hunters, the negroes were taken, in spite of tears and entreaties, to eke out their days in unavailing home-sickness and in bondage. It must have pierced the hearts of many a good Methodist to read in his weekly newspaper such a typical advertisement as the following, which we copy from the *New York Daily Gazette* of March 30, 1789, the very copy, indeed, in which appears Washington's great speech which he addressed to Congress as the newly-elected President.

[4] H. G. Wells, *op. cit.*, p. 466.

'For sale, a likely, healthy, young negro wench, between fifteen and sixteen years old. She has been used to the farming business. Sold for want of employ. Enquire at No. 81, Witham St.'

'Man's inhumanity to man' is the universal reproach of our race. But even more surprising than this, is the indifference to the sorrows of the unfortunate negro, on the part of those who called themselves followers of Him who came to seek and to save that which was lost.

Sir Josiah Stamp says, 'Now take this picture: "How sweet the name of Jesus sounds." What a hymn ! What depths of spiritual insight and knowledge ! What intimacy ! What immediacy ! Something that can sound the depths of experience through the ages. Now see the writer of it—a captain of his ship, singing hymns in his cabin, holding prayer meetings, putting down swearing amongst the crew, and underneath him all the time, a weltering, sweltering mass of African negroes herded under conditions that we should not tolerate for the lowest animals.'[1]

Happily it is not any part of our task here to pursue the sad story of the slave, or to consider the problem which his coloured descendants have created in the United States. 'It is an abyss,' says a present day writer, 'into which we can only look with terror.'[2]

The restlessness within the Church broke out in continual protest and occasional secession. In 1843, for example, the 'Wesleyan Methodist Church' of America was formed of a membership which prohibited slavery, abolished episcopacy and urged simplicity in

[1] *Criticism: and other Addresses*, p. 99.
[2] Siegfried, *America Comes of Age*, p. 108.

THE SUNDERED CHURCH 171

dress and conduct. With a membership to-day of 23,000, it has held on its way.

For other reasons, other secessions had taken place. It was an age of division. There is an uncanny resemblance in the striving and subsequent secessions of that time between American and English Methodism. The Conferences in America had become 'more and more a clerical preserve.'[1] Hence it was that after much agitation and distress the 'Methodist Protestant Church' came into being. The distinctive feature of this secession Church was that it introduced laymen into the legislative Councils. This Church, with its 195,000 members, can claim at least to have led where other Methodist Churches have since followed. But there is no need that we should here give an account of the numerous divisions which took place about this time; the well-nigh score of Methodist denominations in America to-day tells its own sad story. We can only recall its resemblance to our own quarrels of 1847 to 1850, when 'the parent Church in England lost in five years,' says Dr. Fitchett, 'more than Wesley gained in fifty.'[2]

It was slavery, however, that was to make the supreme cleavage, dividing Methodism into Northern and Southern Churches; a division which has remained to this day; and, to our great regret, shows even now no immediate sign of being healed. The story of the upheaval which thus rent Methodism into two halves, is one which should be told with sympathetic restraint. We should maintain a firm resolve to hold the scales evenly, as between the idealists of the North, who were prepared to force an issue, especially when they

[1] *New History of Methodism*, Vol. II. p. 128.
[2] *Wesley and His Century*, p. 528.

were the least affected, and the leaders of the South, who had every day to consider the insuperable difficulties which seemed to emerge if the demands of the North were conceded.

The problem was one of the most perplexing any Church has ever had to face. How could a Christian man, it was argued, buy and sell his fellow man, and keep him in a bondage which denied to him the elementary birthright of every member of God's family ? So the case was stated by the Methodists generally of the Northern States. But in the South, custom and commerce, familiarity and practical politics, seemed to make all talk of emancipation as a condition of Churchmanship simply irrelevant.

The controversy shook the very foundations. The cause at issue was not merely a question of doctrine or of Church government, it was one which raised moral questions of the gravest kind. An error of intellect might result in ex-communication : but the person so excluded could hold up his head and plead his cause to eager and tolerant people, who would not be slow to give their firm approval and benediction. The slave-holder, however, was charged with a sin against God and his fellow man. By some he was regarded almost as a moral outcast. He was stamped with disapproval by the people who spoke in the name of religion. It was this sharp cleavage in sympathy which resulted, first in anger and then in resolute division. Good men felt the charge levelled against them, as though they had been stung with scorpions. The very resentment was of a kind which obscured any gleams of light, which otherwise might have begun to pierce the clouds.

The anger was the more deep because the North,

THE SUNDERED CHURCH 173

which now claimed to be a friend of the slave, and the advocate of his emancipation, had not always shown such moral sensitiveness. It was recalled that, when the slave traffic was a profitable business, the North had not been slow to take part. What right, therefore, had they now to assume the role of moral censor? Their own record required a justification before they undertook to lecture the less fortunate South. Thus the happiness of Methodism gave place to storm and stress. Other questions, it is true, were mixed up with slavery, and added to the bitterness and confusion. The large powers of the bishop and the denial to the layman of a place in the councils of the Church, were questions which had not the geographical limitations of slavery. The agitation on these, and other controversial subjects, all helped to create a desolating atmosphere of fierce debate and mutual recrimination. It was the day of controversy. We may find it hard now to understand how men could have quarrelled as Christians did in those days, both in America and England, or having quarrelled, should break off their relations with the Church of their parents, and set up, in proud defiance, a new denomination.

The division between North and South gradually deepened, and feelings became more intense and more irreconcilable with each succceding year. The rupture which had menaced the great Church for some years was precipitated at last by the case of Bishop James O. Andrew, of the South. It was stated at the General Conference of 1844 that he was a slave owner. This called for comment and legislation. A committee was appointed to make inquiries and submit a report. The Committee set to work at once; in two days they had completed their inquiry and were ready with their findings. A letter from Bishop Andrew was incorporated. Both the terms and the tone of the letter should have prevented the Conference from the hasty step of the next day. Bishop Andrew told the whole story of his relationship with slavery in terms of absolute simplicity. The sum total of his offence was, first, a mulatto girl had been bequeathed to him, but he had been training her with parental care, with a view to her liberty and her return to Liberia. ' I have been made a slave-holder legally but not with my consent.' Secondly, a slave boy had become his property through the death of a relative. He was forbidden by the law to emancipate the boy in his own State : but ' he shall be at liberty to leave the State, whenever I shall be satisfied that he is prepared to provide for himself.' Thirdly, he had married a lady, whose former husband owned slaves. These he would not own, and being unable to liberate, he secured them to his wife by deed of trust. ' I have neither bought nor sold a slave. I have plainly stated all the facts of the case.' To this entirely frànk statement, certain implacable members of the Conference replied by a resolution, that the bishop ' be, and is hereby affectionately asked to resign.' The bishop, it seems, would have been glad to lay down his episcopal honours and office, for he was without ambition, and anxious only to avoid injury to the Church. But there were others who saw that the submission to such a demand was devastating. It carried with it the bulwarks. Feeling can hardly be said to have run high ; there was a noble and most notable restraint. Not an angry word was spoken. Indeed it must occur to most readers of the proceedings, that few controversies in the whole history of the

THE SUNDERED CHURCH 175

Church, which cut so immediately to the very centre of belief and practice, have been so elevated and nobly Christian in tone. This may be interpreted both as a tribute to the spiritual status of the distressed members of the Conference, and itself accepted as a reason why the spiritual progress of the divided Church was not seriously arrested. But the issue was joined, and there was no escape from a sad and deep division. The South saw that if the bishop desisted from his office as he was asked to do, and as he was willing to do, not only would he suffer an injustice, but a principle would be affirmed which unchurched them all. If it was wrong for a bishop to keep slaves, it would be wrong for an elder to do so ; and in the same way it would be wrong for any minister to do so. And, since there is not one moral law for a minister, and another for the layman, the resolution would bring all under condemnation. Even though we may be sure, as of course we are, that slavery was intensely wrong, thousands of good Christian people of that day no more recognized it as such than we recognize the sin of keeping little children in unspeakable hovels, half-fed, half-clothed, and without a glint of beauty in the little bit of the world they can see. Then, even if slavery were wrong, as we have seen, many of these Methodists lived in States, as in Georgia, for instance, where it was illegal to liberate them. So it was that the friends of Bishop Andrew begged him not to resign. If he did so, how could they go back among the slave-holders who were members of their Church ? It is said, indeed, that 25,000 members between them owned not less than 208,000 slaves. How then could the Conference justify this severe and isolated step without appreciating what must follow in its train ?

The end was a dramatic and as it appears to us a deplorable one. A proposal was made, in good spirit, that the Church should divide. It was an easy way out of a difficulty, but the easy way out of a difficulty is seldom the right one. A Plan of Separation was drawn up, which provided for a clear and firm line to be drawn between North and South. The Southerners would create their own organization, and hold their own Conference. The step was taken : the great Church was divided. The Southern portion was to be known, as it is known to this day, as the Methodist Episcopal Church South, while the North retained the title of the Methodist Episcopal Church.

Here we reach a natural, if sombre, point, at which our story may be concluded. Ever since that fateful day the two mighty Churches have pursued their tasks, with the same quenchless zeal, and the same loyalty to evangelical truth. The worst consequences of division, which are wilful overlapping and a contemptuous competition, have been largely avoided, by means of the territorial assignments agreed upon from the first. More than once the two Churches have looked towards each other with a love which kindles in the eyes of those who are of one parentage. Time has laid its gentle and healing hand upon old sores. To bring together these two Churches will require an abundant measure of the grace of our Lord Jesus Christ. It is easier to divide than to unite. Questions which will tax the statesmanship of both Churches must confront those who undertake the thrilling task of bringing them once more into the holy fellowship of a single Church. That day will

THE SUNDERED CHURCH 177

surely come; and with it we may expect will come also the union of other and smaller Methodist denominations in the States. We, on this side of the Atlantic, shall watch for each sign of union with eager eyes, and pray that when it comes, it may be as complete, and as happy, as the union so recently achieved in our own land.

When, for a moment, our minds travel back to that evening in 1766, when Barbara Heck, with a noble challenge, flung the pack of cards into the fire, and stirred up Philip Embury to preach, and watch the heaven-sent succession of men who took up that challenge and carried the gospel to the needy people; when we recall their privations, their zeal, and their heroism; and finally, when we see a Church of such mighty proportions slowly arising, we know that we are looking upon a movement born and directed by the Holy Spirit of God. However long delayed may be the reunion of the Methodist Churches in America, we have an inward assurance that they will be faithful to their great heritage. Thus they will continue to be one of the most potent factors to mould, to chasten and inspire a great nation, whose serious task it must be to face and solve some of the fiercest problems that ever confronted the sons of men.

STATISTICS OF AMERICAN METHODISM TO-DAY.

Denomination.	Ministers.	Lay Preachers.	Church Members and Probationers.	Sunday Schools.	Officers and Teachers.	Sunday Scholars.	Churches, &c.
Methodist Episcopal	20,040	13,585	4,658,862	31,527	394,865	4,375,698	26,732
Methodist Episcopal, South	8,127	4,329	2,621,900	15,339	175,740	1,930,552	17,272
Methodist Protestant	2,175	—	195,460	1,850	17,351	181,373	2,218
African Methodist Episcopal (coloured)	7,315	—	781,692	7,200	—	320,000	7,390
African Methodist Episcopal Zion (Coloured)	3,460	—	500,000	2,429	45,087	267,141	3,882
Coloured Methodist Episcopal	3,208	216	467,520	2,964	23,020	310,210	3,101
Free Methodist	1,399	—	40,827	—	—	—	1,279
Wesleyan Methodist	700	474	23,000	584	6,110	43,632	650
Primitive Methodist	90	73	23,000	87	383	14,600	85
Congregational Methodist	487	—	21,050	80	—	4,807	357
New Congregational Methodist	25	—	1,229	3	—	126	26
Union American Methodist Episcopal (Coloured)	324	—	22,259	—	—	—	307
African Union Methodist Protestant (Coloured)	675	—	27,000	42	273	2,581	650
Reformed Zion Union Apostolic (Col.)	43	—	4,086	36	212	1,500	58
Reformed Methodist Un. Episcopal (Coloured)	51	—	1,904	15	—	400	27
Coloured Methodist Protestant	33	—	533	24	125	1,016	3
Reformed Methodist Church	14	—	401	—	—	—	14
Independent African Meth. Episcopal	—	—	1,003	—	—	—	29
	48,166	18,677	9,391,726	62,180	663,166	7,453,636	64,080

INDEX

Abbott, Benjamin, 97f
  Asbury's tribute to, 98
Adams, John, 57
Addison, Joseph, 27
Aldersgate Street, Wesley at,
  21, 29
American Methodism—
  First Society formed in New
    York, 50f
  rapid growth of, 60f, 138f,
    141
  first Methodist Chapel built,
    61ff
  appeals to English Methodism, 64ff, 67f, 71f, 78
  Society classes introduced,
    82f
  relations with English Methodism, 82f
  rules for Preachers, 83f
  effect of Revolution on, 86ff
  dangers of division, 101ff
  love of learning in, 164f
  division into Northern and
    Southern sections, 171ff,
    176
  reunion of, 176f
  statistics of, 178
    (*see also* Methodist
    Episcopal Church refs.)
'American Methodism' (Dr.
  Stevens), *see* refs. to Dr.
  Stevens
American Revolution—
  causes, 86f
  effect on English Missionaries,
    88f
  end of, 95
  effect on American Methodism, 95
Andrew, Bishop James O.,
  173f

Asbury, Francis—
  designated to America, 72
  quoted, 73, 76, 113, 118, 126,
    137, 143, 151, 166
  early days, 73f
  appointed Assistant or Superintendent of American
    Societies, 75
  industry, 76, 92
  passion for prayer, 76f, 92
  in Philadelphia and Baltimore, 78
  superseded by Rankin, 80f
  requested to return to
    England, 81f
  in Norfolk, Virginia, 82
  decides to remain in America
    during Revolution, 89f,
    91f
  love of learning, 92ff, 95, 142,
    163
  journeys of, 76ff, 139
  Journal of, 92
  influence on Methodist Universities, 94
  appointed General Superintendent in America, 95f
  tribute to Abbott, 98
  question of Sacraments, 101ff
  meets Dr. Coke, 117
  ordained Joint-Superintendent with Coke, 120
  visits General Washington,
    127f, 129f
  dress of, 136
  Cokesbury College, 142f
  his stationing of Preachers,
    145f
  celibacy, 149ff
  affection for children, 151
  Boehm's description of, 152
  illnesses of, 74, 139, 147

INDEX

Asbury, Francis—(continued)
death and burial (at Baltimore), 152f
President Coolidge's eulogy of, 152f
Ashton, 54

Baltimore, General Conferences at, first (1784), 119, 132, 141; second (1792), 133, 138, 141; third (1800), 148; fourth (1808), 157f
Baltimore, Lord (Founder of Maryland), 17f
Bangs, Dr. Nathan, quoted, 157f
Baptism and Lord's Supper, see Sacraments
Bett, Rev. Henry, Studies in Literature, quoted, 113
Bishop, title of, adopted in Methodism, 122f
Boardman, Richard, 67f
in New York, 69
letter to Wesley, 70
returns to England, 84
Boehm, Henry, 148
description of Asbury, 152
Book of Common Prayer, Wesley's treatment of, 136
Bourne, F. W., James Thorne, quoted, 163
Brayshaw, The Quakers, quoted, 167
Bristol Conference (1768), 64ff
Burke, Edmund, quoted, 87f, 90

Cabot, John, discovered Newfoundland, 15
Cadman, Dr. Parkes, quoted, 20
Camp Meetings, 161ff
Carlyle, quoted, 89
Cartwright, Peter, 160
Finley's tribute to, 160f
autobiography, quoted, 162f
Charles I, 17, 19
Charleston Hymn Book, 27

Coke, Dr.—
dismissed from Church of England, 107
ordained by Wesley as Superintendent of work in America, 108f
lands at New York, 117
meets Asbury, 117
travels, 119, 125, 126
visits General Washington, 127f, 129f
returns to England, 129
returns to America, 133
relations with Asbury, 138
Cokesbury College, founded, 142ff
a failure, 143f
Coolidge, President, tribute to Asbury, 152f
Cooper, Ezekiel, quoted, 117f
Creighton, Rev. James, 108

Declaration of Independence, 19, 85
Delamotte, Charles, 26, 34
Dickens, John, 120f

Early Methodist Preachers, Lives of, quoted, 36f, 80
Edwards, Jonathan, 36, 42
Embury, Philip, builds preaching house at Ballingarane, 49
leaves for America, 49
zeal, 65
founds Society at Ashgrove, 70
death of, 70
Emigrants, Early, 15f
Encyclopædia Britannica, quoted, 19, 42
English Methodism, American appeals to, 64ff, 71f
Evans, Edward, 39

Finley, J. B., quoted, 160f, 162
Fitchett, Dr., quoted, Wesley and his Century, 171
Forsyth, The Church and Sacraments, quoted, 100

INDEX 181

Franklin, Benjamin, 36, 42, quoted, 46

Garrettson, Freeborn, 99, 118
conversion of, 121f
Gatch, Philip, 97
General Conferences at Baltimore, first (1784), 119, 132, 141; second (1792), 133, 138, 141; third (1800), 148; fourth (1808), 157f
George III, 86, 88
Georgia—
founded, 19
General Oglethorpe, first Governor, 24
Wesley in, 26ff
Wesley leaves, 31
Whitefield offers for, 34
poverty and disease in, 40
slavery in, 44
German hymns, translated by John Wesley, 27
German Methodists in Ireland, 48ff
Gilbert, Sir Humphrey, 13
Gladstone, quoted, 16
Gladstone, George Whitefield, M.A., Field Preacher, quoted, 43
Green, John Richard, quoted, 13, 18

Heck, Barbara—
leaves for America, 49
stirs Philip Embury to preach so that first Methodist Society is formed in New York, 50f, 61f, 177
Heck, Paul, 49
Hopkey, Miss S., 30
Howard, Dr., quoted, 145f

Ingham, Benjamin, 26

James I, 15, 16, 18
James, Duke of York (later James II), 19, 60
John Street Chapel, New York, 61ff

Johnson, Dr. Samuel, 90f
Journal of Asbury, 92
Journal of John Wesley, quoted, 31, 50, 56f

King, John, 61
King, Lord, Account of the Primitive Church and its effect on Wesley, 106ff
Kingsley, Charles, quoted, 14f

Laud, Archbishop, 17, 16, 18
Lecky, criticism of Whitefield, 42
Lee, Jesse, 148
Leeds Conference (1769), 67f
designates Boardman and Pilmoor for America, 67
Lewis, quoted, 123, 135
Lincoln, Abraham, quoted, 166
Lives of Early Methodist Preachers, John Nelson, quoted, 36f, 80
Lord's Supper and Baptism, see Sacraments
Lowth, Bishop of London, refuses to ordain Hoskin, 104ff

Maine, and New England, 18
Maryland, 17f
Methodism in, 52f
Pilmoor at, 70
Maryland Methodism unites with Methodism in New York, 70f
Masefield, John, The Everlasting Mercy, quoted, 48
McKendree, Bishop, 147
care of Asbury, 151, 155
conversion, 155
description of, 156
elected Bishop, 156f
preaching, 157ff
Methodist Colleges and Universities, their debt to Francis Asbury, 94, 163ff
(see Cokesbury College)
Methodist Episcopal Church—
born in Baltimore, 119f
growth of, 125, 126ff

INDEX

Methodism Episcopal Church—
(*continued*)
  secessions from, 146, 170f
  division into Northern and Southern sections, 171ff, 176
  See American Methodism
Methodist Protestant Church, 171
Milton, *Areopagitica*, quoted, 86, 140
Moravians, 26, 28, 37
Morley, *Life of Gladstone*, quoted, 44

Narrative of the Life of Whitefield, quoted, 41, 45
Nelson, John, quoted, 21, 36f, 80
New England, settlement of Puritans in, 18f
  education in, 19f
Newfoundland, discovered, 15
New History of Methodism, quoted, 55f, 69, 84, 136, 158, 171
New York Daily Gazette, quoted, 128
New York Methodism—
  beginnings, 50ff, 61
  unites with Methodism in Maryland, 70f
New York State, 19, 60, 61
  John Street Chapel built in, 61ff
  Boardman arrives in, 69
  Conference at, 130, 133
North, Lord, 86, 88

Oglethorpe, General—
  first Governor of Georgia, 24
  persuades Wesley to go to Georgia, 25f, 30
  attitude to slavery, 44
O'Kelly, James, 121, 138, 144f
  resignation of, 146
  ordination, 102
Otis, James, 88

Palatines, 49
  poverty of, 49f
  leave for America, 49, 50
Penn, William, 19
Pennsylvania, 19
Philadelphia, first Methodist Conference, July 14, 1773, 55, 82
  Pilmoor arrives in, 69
Pilgrim Fathers, 18
Pilmoor, Joseph, 67f
  at Philadelphia, 69
  in Maryland, 70
  preaching, 71
  returns to England, 84
Puritans, settlement in America, 18

Quakers, settle in Pennsylvania, 19
  attitude to slavery, 167
Quinn, James, quoted, 137

Rankin, Thomas—
  tribute to Whitefield, 36f
  quoted, 73, 81
  appointed to America, 78
  succeeds Asbury, 79, 80
  conversion, 79f
  meets Wesley, 79f
  returns to England, 89
Republican Methodist Church, formation of, 146f
Ruff, Daniel, 98f

Sacraments, American preachers forbidden to administer, 83f, 95, 96, 101,
  dangers of division over question of, 101ff
Shadford, George, appointed to America, 78
  Wesley's letter to, 78f
  returns to England, 89f
Siegfried, *America comes of Age*, quoted, 170
Simon, *John Wesley the Master Builder*, quoted, 60
Slavery, 96, 127ff, 166ff
  Methodist attitude to, 167

INDEX 183

Slave —(continued)
  Wesley's attitude to, 44, 168
  New Testament in relation to, 168
  English attitude to, 169
  cruelty of, 169f
  divides American Methodism, 171ff
Southern Colonies, religious communities in, 20
Southey, Robert, quoted, 98, 112
Spangenberg (Moravian), 28f
Stamp, Sir J., quoted, 170
Stevens, Dr. Abel, American Methodism, quoted, 42, 54, 55, 61, 70, 75, 76, 77, 84, 103, 122, 124, 126f, 129, 137, 156
Strawbridge, Robert, 52
  preaching, 53
  death and burial, 54
  attitude to Sacraments, 100f

Taylor, Thomas, letter to Wesley, 64ff
Tyerman, *Life of George Whitefield*, quoted, 38, 46, 111, 168

Vasey, Mr., 108
  ordained Elder, 110
Virginia, 16f
  first Methodist circuit in, 55

Washington, General, visited by Asbury and Coke, 127f, 129f
  letter to, 130f
  reply of, 131f
  attitude to slavery, 167f
Watters, William, 96f
Watts, Isaac, 27
Webb, Captain, 56ff
  returns to England, 84
  death and burial, 84f
Wells, H. G., quoted, 128, 169
Wesley, Charles, leaves for Georgia, 26
  returns to England, 28

Wesley, Charles—(continued)
  attitude to ordination of Methodist Preachers, 107
  quoted, 154
Wesley, John—
  conversion, 21f
  Whitefield's tribute to his work in Georgia, 22f
  father's death, 23f
  sails for Georgia, 26
  meets the Moravians, 26, 28
  Translates German hymns, 27
  composes Charlestown Hymn Book, 27
  friendship with Miss Hopkey, 30
  returns to England, 31
  attitude to slavery, 44, 168
  in Ireland, Balingarane, 48f, 50
  tribute to Captain Webb, 57
  letter to George Shadford, 78f
  A Calm Address to the American People, 90f
  question of Sacraments in America, 104f
  request to Lowth, Bishop of London, 104ff
  effect of Lord King's *Account of the Primitive Church* on, 106ff
  decides to ordain Methodist Preachers, 106
  'sets apart' Dr. Coke, 108
  letters to American Methodists, 109f, 114f
  views on Apostolic succession, 111f
  letters to Asbury, 123, 142
  name dropped from and restored to American Methodist Conference Minutes, 134f
  Asbury's tribute on the death of, 137
Wesley, Susanna (Mother of John and Charles Wesley), 26

INDEX

Wesleyan Methodist Church of America, formed, 170f
Whatcoat, Richard, 108
　ordained Elder, 110, 134
　ordained Bishop, 148f
White, Judge, 90
Whitefield, George—
　tribute to Wesley's work in America, 22f, 39
　offers for missionary work, 34
　early life, 34
　preacher and evangelist, 35f, 41ff, 45
　sails for America, 37
　work in America, 38ff
　relations with Methodism, 38, 39
　philanthropist, 39ff

Whitefield, George—(*continued*)
　builds Orphan house, 40f
　Lecky's criticism of, 42
　industry, 42ff
　attitude to slavery, 44f
　his will, 45
　travels, 38, 46
　death and burial, 47
Whittier, *quoted*, 33
Williams, Robert, 54f
　Asbury's tribute to, 55
　forbidden to publish books, 84
Wright, Richard, 72
　returns to England, 84

Xavier, Life of, influence on Dr. Coke, 116